D1391381

COX'S
FRAGMENTA

COX'S
FRAGMENTA
AN HISTORICAL
MISCELLANY

EDITED BY SIMON MURPHY

The
History
Press

© British Library Board. All Rights Reserved 937.g.1–94.
All illustrations courtesy of Lillian Low.

First published 2010

The History Press
The Mill, Brimscombe Port
Stroud, Gloucestershire, GL5 2QG
www.thehistorypress.co.uk

© Simon Murphy for selection and editorial matter, 2010

The right of Simon Murphy to be identified as the Editor
of this work has been asserted in accordance with the
Copyrights, Designs and Patents Act 1988.

British Library Cataloguing in Publication Data.
A catalogue record for this book is available from the British Library.

ISBN 978 0 7524 5171 8

Typesetting and origination by The History Press
Printed in India
Manufacturing managed by Jellyfish Print Solutions Ltd

To the conductor of the *Sun*,

Sir,

If an inhabitant of some remote Country, totally uninformed of the Political business of this, but sufficiently skilled in the English language to read the newspapers, was to come into this country, and resort to the public prints for information respecting its Government, Laws, People, &c. &c. it may not be incurious to consider what in all probability his opinion of them would be. I think, then, that it is probable that he would in the first place set it down as a certainty, that the minds of the people were in general but as so many blank sheets, for fools and designing men to scribble what absurdities they pleased upon; so that the Government was of little other use than to furnish a topic for the abusive pens of Grub-street Garreteers; that its magistrates served only as objects of invective for the factious scribblers of the day; and that its Laws were either in themselves inefficient, or their Executive Officers supinely negligent in the execution of them.

Senex

~

INTRODUCTION

The *Fragmenta* must be one of the stranger texts to lurk in the depths of the British Library; a leviathan composed of ninety-four folio volumes, each volume containing well over 200 pages, each page featuring disparate clippings from the newspapers of Birmingham and London ordered in a chaotic chronology from the late 1750s through to 1833. The topics that jostle alongside one another vary enormously, stretching from warfare to weevils, from cricket to crime, and from modes of courtship common in Fife to frog-inhabited barometers. All in all, the collection takes up over 20ft of shelving, and is the work – so far as we know – of a single man. Un-indexed, un-indexable and scarcely annotated, it defies interpretation and conventional scholarship. Francis Cox's enigmatic collection simply begs the question – Why?

A brief survey of the origin and provenance of the work elicits no straightforward answers. We know Francis Cox lived from 1752 to 1834 and plied his trade

first in Birmingham and later in London as either
a linen draper or a brush maker. He was married
with two daughters. Few other facts about his life
are recorded, and in truth it is unlikely we would be
aware of Cox today, were it not for the curious clause
in his will (written in August 1834) in which can be
found the first extant reference to his magnum opus:

> Moreover should the volumes called the
> Fragmenta be in my possession at the time of my
> death consisting of one hundred folio volumes for
> which I have been collecting for upwards of half a
> century be deemed worthy the acceptance of the
> Governors I leave devise and bequeath them to the
> Museum in Russell St. Bloomsbury.

Cox died a little over a month later, and his widow
Sarah wrote to the governors to inform them of her
late husband's wish, asking only that she be granted
time to look over the collection before it was
received by the Museum. Examining the collection
became – rather unsurprisingly given its scale – a
much more formidable undertaking than she had
anticipated, and it was not until August of the
following year that the *Fragmenta* finally entered

the collection of the Museum's library (now the British Library), as a ninety-four-volume set.[1] And there it has quite patiently remained for the last 175 years, during which time only two things of any interest have occurred to it.

Firstly it was re-catalogued in 1922, when the volumes were (mis)entered under the following description:

> Burney (Charles) DD: A collection of miscellaneous cuttings from newspapers, made for Burney and continued after his death.

The sudden link to the Reverend Charles Burney (1757–1817) makes a strange sort of sense. Burney was a classical scholar and bibliophile, conspicuous during his youth for dismissal from Gonville and Caius College under charges of pilfering books from the Cambridge library and replacing the university arms with his own. His sister later suggested that this lapse in his judgement was due to a 'mad rage to possess a library', though

---

1. And not the 100 stated by Cox's will. It is perhaps possible that the century was a target he had presaged (with an eye to his advancing age) as a suitable place to conclude.

others have suggested he sold the books to cover mounting gambling debts. In either case, Burney eventually did gather together an astounding library containing over 13,000 printed books and 500 manuscript volumes, bought by the British Museum in 1818 for the princely sum of £13,500. The collection was valuable, not only for its many classical editions, but also for the collection of newspapers it contained. Burney's maiden aunts managed 'Gregg's-Coffee-House', and from 1781 they collected the papers for him. These have recently been digitised by the British Library.

Given this mutual conviction of the present and future significance of newspapers, it is not difficult to see how a cataloguer might have considered Cox's horde as an extension of Burney's collection, and indeed the strange wording of Cox's will, 'should the volumes called the Fragmenta be in my possession at the time of my death', suggests he half-expected them to be retrieved by another party. Despite the impulse to connect Cox to such an interesting figure, there are no solid ties linking the men. Their divergent methodologies – Cox cut the papers to single articles, often divesting them of both date and imprint, whereas Burney left them whole – also mark the collections as separate endeavours.

The second event of note occurred in 1966 when leading librarian and bibliographer C.B. Oldman wrote a survey of Cox and his collection. That Oldman's ten-page commentary remains to this day the definitive (and only) work is entirely to his credit, but also perhaps hints at the genuine obscurity of Cox. Despite the efforts of Oldman, the ninety-four volumes are all that Cox seems to have left us – at least for the present.

My first contact with the text was during a seminar at the British Library, when a friend flipped open volume seventeen at random and after a brief snort of baffled laughter read aloud:

> Tuesday the Otter hounds of Mr. Coleman of Leominster, killed in Monkland mill-pond, an otter of extraordinary size; it measured from the nose to the end of the tail four feet ten inches, and weighed 34½lb. This animal was supposed to be nearly 8 years old, and to have destroyed a ton of fish yearly.

I was hooked. The dubious yet purported accuracy of the figures, coupled with such questionable newsworthiness, lent the excerpt a kind of bathos. The archaic language ('otter hounds') set the article as utterly removed from the papers of today, yet the all-pervasive obsession with extremes ('biggest', 'longest', 'most costly') depicted human nature at its most nosey, vicarious and banal, and what's more, reveal it as historically constant. As temporally distant readers of Cox's collection we can go one further than the 'inhabitant of the remote country' postulated by Senex: we can scour the newspapers for the idiosyncrasies of time, as well as place. The past may well be a foreign country, but surely there can be few more unique or amusing ways of comprehending an era than to sit down to breakfast with the crumbs of its papers.

≈

NOTE ON THE TEXT

A word of warning. This selection is to be read with a pinch of salt, lest the mind of the reader unfortunately become one more 'blank sheet, for fools and designing men to scribble what absurdities they pleased upon'. The reliability of reports may occasionally have been impaired by an editor's earnest desire to get a fresh story out to the street, or by a hurried typesetter trying to squeeze a late slug onto the chase … and occasionally inaccuracies may have crept in lacking such honest excuses. The competition was often first to point the finger: 'On Saturday night the Jacobean *Evening-Echo* obtruded upon the Public a letter dated *Manheim* July 31 – thus this *wonderful Print* receives Dispatches from the distance of near 1300 miles in 48 hours!!' (v.9, p.52) – as shocking as it once would have been.

It seems such rivalries extended beyond the printed page, and onto the street:

CAUTION – We have received intimation from several Friends and correspondents, that a scheme is nightly practiced by the Vendors of a Paper called the *Courier*, to injure the sales of THE SUN. These vendors procure all the old papers of THE SUN they can get, and then damp them ready for their purpose; and after it is dark, if any person ask them for this paper their answer is 'Don't you want a *Courier* ...?'

The Sun, c. 1793 (v.8, p.8)

But newspapers were not beyond a little gaiety, and occasionally made light of their own less-than-spotless reputations. The following excerpt was taken from a comic interlude called *The Drunken News-Writer*, performed at the Theatre Royal in Haymarket in 1770. A paper chose to print the scene in which the news-writer enters, drunk, and settles to his business:

Let me see – Yes! Like a wise Caterer, I'll collect the best materials from the *other* Papers, that I may serve the more elegant OLIO in my own. (*sits down and prepares to read the Papers*), the *Public Advertiser* – right! I like to take things according to

order – the *Public Advertiser* is like – what? – Egad,
it is like a MADE DISH – full of *good things,* and
of the most *opposite* qualities. Yes! – The *Public
Ledger* is *water gruel*, without *salt* or *butter* – and
has neither *flavour* nor *substance*. – The *Gazetteer*,
– or, *The New Daily Advertiser*, – is like an *unfilled
hogshead* – full of *sound*, and empty: – And the
Daily Advertiser – pardon, O ye sons of Trade, if
I call the *Daily* a *Basket of chips* – for it is *dry*, and fit
for the fire. And so having finished my digression,
let me see what these dispatches bring – (*reads*)
'The following may be depended on as *authentic*,'
– Pfhaw! that's a *lie* – for I wrote it myself.

(v.4, p.102)

So, now the reader is accordingly warned about the
content of the following, I should briefly outline
how such a short selection was made from such a
vast collection. The short answer is with difficulty
and partiality. An attempt was made to derive a
method based on one of the rare marked articles
in the collection, which perhaps provides an
indication of Cox's own interest as he read. The
excerpt is from *The Times*, on Tuesday 13 August
1822 (v.53, p.243), and relates the events leading

up to the suicide of the Marquis of Londonderry. Cox first indicates (with a vertical ink line in the margin) a section which reads:

> For the laſt ten days, the Marquis had been suffering under a nervous fever, accompanied by a depression of ſpirits. On Friday he underwent the operation of cupping; after which, it appeared that his fever did not increase, though no alteration in the ſtate of mind was perceptible, he ſtill being subjeċt to deſpondency.

This would be a perfectly natural section of the text to stress; however, further down there is another mark – one far less simple to explain. A great ink cross near the foot picks out a single sentence: 'We understand, however, that he rose as early as seven o'clock yesterday morning, and drank a cup of tea and ate a muffin, before the fatal event took place.' The inanity of the breakfast of the suicide seemed of more interest to Cox than the incident itself.

Francis Cox's selection displays a wide-ranging interest in the politics, sports and entertainments of his day, but it also suggests he had an eye for the comic turn, the absurd, the irregular and occasionally the vulgar. It is this off-the-wall quality that I have attempted to retain in this selection, hoping that in doing so, Cox's fragments might receive some long-overdue attention, but also that, in some sense, the unique *personality* the collection implies can endure.

This collection covers roughly the first half of Cox's ninety-four volumes. Should it prove popular enough, a second part may well be produced.

Variant spellings have been retained throughout, and articles may occasionally have been subject to judicious editing for reasons of space.

~

STONE EATER

The beginning of May, 1760, was brought to
Avignon a true Lithophagus, or stone eater. This
not only swallows flints of an inch and a half
long, a full inch broad, and half an inch thick; but
such stones as he could reduce to powder, such as
marbles, pebbles, &c. he made up into paste, which
was to him a most agreeable and wholesome food.
I examined this man with all the attention I possibly
could. I found his gullet very large, his teeth
exceeding strong, his saliva very corrosive, and his
stomach lower than ordinary, which I imputed to
the vast number of flints he had swallowed, being
about five-and-twenty one day with another.

Upon interrogating his keeper, he told me the
following particulars: this stone eater, says he, was
found three years ago in a northern uninhabited
island, by some of the crew of a Dutch ship, on
Good Friday. Since I have had him, I make him
eat raw flesh with his stones: I could never get him
to swallow bread. He will drink water, wine, and

brandy; which laſt liquor gives him infinite pleasure. He sleeps at leaſt twelve hours in a day, sitting on the ground with one knee over the other, and his chin reſting on his right knee. The flints he has swallowed he voids somewhat corroded and diminished in weight, the reſt of his excrements resembles mortar.

The Morning Chronicle **and** *London Advertiser*,
Wednesday 26 March 1788 (v.1, p.7)

~

MANNER OF PUNISHING

THOSE GUILTY OF A LIBEL

IN RUSSIA

We complain very heavily of the men who write libels; but the method we take to punish has not the effect which is intended. It does not deter the offenders, nor terrify others from committing the same crime. Imprisonment, pillory, burning the libel, and some other things of the same sort, are what these Gentlemen earnestly desire. It saves them the expense of advertising. They manage things differently in Russia. A gentleman in Petersburgh thought fit to publish a quarto pamphlet, reflecting upon the unlimited power of the Sovereign, and exposing the iniquity with which it was exerted. The offender was immediately seized by virtue of a warrant signed by one of the principle Officers of State, was tried in a summary way, his book determined to be a libel, and he himself, as the author, condemned to EAT HIS OWN WORDS. The sentence was literally carried into execution, a scaffold was erected in the most public street in town, the Imperial Provost was the executioner, and all the inferior Magistrates attended the ceremony. The book was severed from the binding, the margins were cut off, and every leaf was rolled up in the form of a lottery ticket when it is taken out of the wheel at Guildhall. The author was then fed with them separately by the Provost. The gentleman had received a compleat mouthful before he began to chew; but he was obliged, upon pain of the severest bastinado, to swallow as many of the leaves as the attendant surgeon thought it possible for him to do without immediate hazard of his life. In three days the author actually swallowed every leaf of his book, and seemed to feel little uneasiness, except at swallowing some leaves on which were the strongest arguments.

General Evening Post, **Tuesday 10 March 1789 (v.1, p.21)**

A notorious character, lately discharged from Newgate, one night last week, met an attorney in Holborn, whom he seized by the throat, and robbed of twelve shillings and sixpence. He afterwards wished the lawyer (whom he well knew) a good night and told him it was only one thief robbed another.

c. **April 1789 (v.1, p.43)**

The following is a literal copy of an elegant printed Card, which is presented to every new married couple as they come out of a church at the bottom of Holborn:

Honoured Sir and Madam,

We the Parish Bell Ringers present our respects to congratulate your happy marriage, humbly hoping to be *happy* enough ourselves to *receive the favour* as we do from all other gentlefolk as we do on this most happy event. Which is all at present from

Your humble servants,

The Bell Ringers.

N.B. we shall be happy to serve you both, or either, upon any future occasion.

Gazetteer and *New Daily Advertiser*, Friday 1 May 1789 (v.1, p.44)

❖

The volcano which burst out near Ballycaille, in the country of Antrim, on the 30th of May, confirms Dr. Hamilton's opinion, as well as that of many others, that the Giant's Causeway, in that neighbourhood, was a volcanic production, and that the pillars which compose that famous work must have been once liquid basaltes as they are found to contain the exact matter which forms the lava of Vesuvius. This is a new phenomenon in the natural history of Ireland, and may, in some measure, account for the horns of elk and moose deer, of an extraordinary size, so often found in that country; Professor Maupertius, of Berlin, published a treatise which went to prove, that from his having found an obelisk in Lapland, in 76 degrees of north latitude, full of engraved characters, which could not be deciphered, the earth must have changed its situation, and there was a probability that those regions now within the Arctic Circle might once have been under the torrid zone.

[NOTE: The naturalist William Hamilton (1755–1801) published *Letters concerning the northern coast of the county of Antrim … wherein is stated a plain and impartial VIEW of the VOLCANIC THEORY of BASALTES* in 1786. He rejected myths and proposals concerning the formation of the causeway's famously hexagonal basalt columns (some seriously claiming them to be man- or giant-made), siding instead with the well-liked theory that slowly cooling lava fractured in a regular pattern. He described the basalt itself as 'a black, ponderous stone; of uniform close grain, and hard texture, fusible and vitrifiable *per se*; and pretty strongly magnetical. It does not effervesce in any of the mineral acids; it is free from animal or vegetable exuviæ, nor does it contain the slightest vestige of any organised substance whatever.' *Letters* … p.43]

General Evening Post, **Tuesday 10 June 1788 (v.1, p.76)**

There cannot be a greater prostitution of talents, than the appointment of a poet of true genius to the Laureate's office. It is absurd, as to employ Sir Joshua Reynolds to paint Transparencies for a Royal illumination. His majesties Recovery, probably the subject of Mr. Warton's next Birth-day Ode, however splendid and important, is a subject which holds forth no new poetical imagery. It is the province of a common rhymer to celebrate popular topics.

c. **June 1788 (v.1, p.102)**

~

DESCRIPTION OF A
NEW INVENTED FROG
BAROMETER, LATELY
DISCOVERED AT PARIS

Take one of those small green frogs which are to
be found in hedges, put it in a white glass bottle,
the neck of which must be large enough to receive
the little animal *tout a fait a son aise.* Previous to its
being let down, put in the bottle some earth and
water to the height of about four fingers breadth,
and also a little wooden ladder that may reach
from the bottom to the lower part of the neck.
Let the bottle be properly stopped with a piece of
parchment, pricked with a pin so as to admit the
air. As long as the weather continues fair, the frog
stands a-top of the ladder, but goes down into the
water at the approach of rain. You must from time
to time, that is, every week or fortnight, change the

water. Many of these animals have been known to live three years without any food.

The Morning Chronicle and London Advertiser,
Wednesday 24 September 1788 (v.1, p.112)

~

BEANS AND BACON

Phelim O'More was indicted at a county assize, in Ireland, for a rape.

His defence was ingenious. He gave in proof that he had a garden of *beans*, in which the prosecutrix committed, nightly, trespasses and depredations.

That having caught her stealing his *beans*, he declared, if she came again she might expect such consequences as she swore to on trial.

She came, and he kept his word.

The Court were of opinion, that the notice and the trespasses in the *bean* garden purged the act of felony, by showing consent *a priori* in the prosecutrix – and the culprit was *acquitted*.

As he departed from the bar, Mr. Costello, who had been Council against him, said – 'My good friend, you have made a most excellent defence to save your *bacon*, but a very bad one to save your *beans*.'

And it was remarked, that poor Phelim could never afterwards keep his beans in his garden; – 'the women,' as he said, 'would be *after* pulling them and pulling them.'

***Public Advertiser*, Wednesday 26 August 1789 (v.1, p.121)**

❖

The following melancholy accident happened a few days since. A gentleman, who had dined at the Bush, at Staines, and had sacrificed too freely to Bacchus, borrowed a pistol of the waiter, to defend himself against robbers. On his arrival in town he went to a house of ill fame in Long-acre, where he sent for one of those poor creatures, who are so unfortunate as to be at the call of any man who has the appearance of having a guinea in his pocket. Being determined to try if the pistol he had borrowed would have answered the purpose had he been attacked by a highwayman, he pulled the trigger frequently, but it would not go off; at last, he was so convinced that nothing would make it fire, that he put the muzzle two or three times within his mouth; this circumstance so alarmed the poor lady that was with him, that she intreated him not to attempt it again; upon which he said, if she would not permit him to shoot himself he would shoot her, and immediately presented the pistol at her, when it went off, lodging the contents, which were of large shot, in her head; she is not dead, but has lost one eye and part of her skull. She is attended by an eminent surgeon (Cruikshanks), who thinks she may recover. The unhappy woman is named Curtis, and is sister to a celebrated actress.

[NOTE: The press of the time regularly featured horrific (and often rather generic) tales of accidental shootings, published as a caution against the mishandling of guns, and to warn against giving children free rein with firearms. This fragment appears to have some truth to it. The writer and actress Ann Curtis – herself, and not (as reported) her sister – was indeed shot in the eye in the manner described whilst on the premises of a bagnio. However, it is possible the severity of her condition was overstated. In later years she was described as merely a 'coarse, large, ill-shaped creature who squints abominably'. Mrs Mortimer, *Welsh Likenesses*, 3.204.]

Whitehall Evening Post, Saturday 5 December 1789
(v.1, p.139)

≈

EXTRAORDINARY SAGACITY

OF RATS

At Amsterdam, in a street called the Wool-Market, recently lived a man who was curious in keeping fowls. One of his hens, though in the midst of summer, had for several weeks stopped yielding her usual produce, and yet daily made her natural cackling; – he searched her nest but could not even find a shell of an egg, which made him resolve to watch her closely. He accordingly the next day situated himself in such a manner as to observe her motions minutely; when to his great surprise, he saw her discharging an egg – but no sooner was she off her nest, than three Rats made their appearance. One of them immediately laid himself on his back, whilst the others rolled the egg upon his belly, which he clasped between his legs and held it very firm; the other two then laid hold of his tail, and gently dragged him out of sight. This wonderful sagacity was exhibited for several days to some curious observers. A gentleman now in London was an eye witness to the above transaction.

Morning Star, **Monday 7 September 1789**
(v.1, p.140)

~

FOTHERGEL'S DROPS FOR NERVOUS FEVERS, AND EXTREME FEEBLENESS

Relaxations from a long continuance in hot countries, from miscarriages, or difficult labours, or old age, or loss of appetite, bad digestion, restless nights, frightful dreams, desponding thoughts, confused ideas, loss of memory, dorsal consumptions, dimness of sight, pains in the head, from vapours, heaviness, lassitude, weakness, wind, pain in the stomach and bowels, instability of mind, extreme laughing or crying, lowness of spirits, hypochondriac passion, melancholy madness, lethargy, apoplexy, palsy, St. Vitus's dance, falling sickness, hysteria and convulsion fits, dumbness, wandering and fixed gout, dread, horror, fear, debilitated constitutions & etc.

[NOTE: The streets of Georgian England were awash with charlatans and mountebanks promising to cure all ailments from colds to cancers. Some were successful, or at least harmless; others were potentially much more hazardous. Whatever their effect, such 'medicines' (along with dogs, wig-power and gloves) were the subject of duties and taxes. The schedule for the House of Commons, April 1830, records the duty upon 'every packet, box, bottle, pot, phial, or other inclosure containing any of the medicines or compositions hereinafter mentioned and specified, made, prepared, uttered, vended or exposed or kept for sale in any part of the united kingdom'. Alongside Fothergel's the list notes the existence of 'Allan's Nipple Liniment', 'Grimston's Eye Snuff', 'Hallows's Antibilious Pills', 'Miller's Worm Plums' and the rather enigmatic 'Italian Bosom Friend'. *Journal of the House of Commons*, 85, pp.313–19]

Morning Herald, Friday 13 November 1789 (v.1, p.153)

~

LONDON: DUEL BETWEEN

LORD MACARTNEY

AND GENERAL STUART

Yesterday morning a duel was fought near Kensington, between Lord Macartney and Major-general Stuart, of which the following is an authentic account, as transmitted by the Seconds, Colonel Fullarton and Colonel Gordon; the former accompanying Lord Macartney and the latter Major-general Stuart.

The place and time of meeting having been previously fixed, the parties arrived at about half past four o'clock in the morning, and took their ground at a distance of twelve short paces, measured off by the seconds, who delivered to each one a pistol, keeping possession of the remaining arms. General Stuart told Lord Macartney, he doubted, as his Lordship was short sighted, he would be able to see him; his Lordship replied 'he did, perfectly well.' When the seconds had retired a little on one side, and the parties were about to level, General Stuart observed to Lord Macartney that his pistol was not cocked, his lordship thanked him, and cocked. When they had levelled, General Stuart said he was ready; his lordship answered; he was likewise ready, and they both fired within a few seconds of each other. The seconds, observing Lord Macartney wounded, stepped up to him and observed that the matter must rest here.

[NOTE: Lord Macartney was no stranger to notoriety. He toured Europe during his youth, meeting and befriending both Rousseau and Voltaire. In 1767 he was named ambassador to Russia but shortly withdrew, having seduced two Russian court ladies and besmirched his character. During a political career that continued to take him abroad, he travelled to India, the Cape, Peking, Verona, Tobago, Ulster, Grenada and Madras. The duel was fought over Macartney's dismissal of Stuart from Madras for incompetence.]

Morning Post and *Daily Advertiser*, **Friday 9 June 1791 (v.2, p.2)**

~

SLAVE TRADE

The advocates of the slave trade are endeavouring to irritate the public mind on the subject, by representing the proposal for an abolition as a questionto be contended by parties and sects. It is, however, a question of common justice, common humanity, and common sense.

c. 1792 (v.2, p.126)

~

BIRMINGHAM

A great number of the inhabitants of this town abstain from sugar and rum, as the most likely means of abolishing the Slave Trade.

The following question was discussed on Monday last, at the society for free debate: 'Are we justifiable in consuming sugar or rum, which we know are produced by the assistance of slaves?' A very genteel and numerous company attended, and though there were some strong advocates for the use of sugar and rum, yet it was decided against them by a very great majority.

Some unknown enemy to slavery caused several hundred pamphlets to be given to those who attended, in which the miseries of slavery were exhibited in lively colours, and deductions made attempting to prove, that those who used sugar or rum were as guilty of flagellation and murder as those who were actually employed in that abominable trade.

The Star, **Monday 26 December 1791 (v.3, p.9)**

To the Printers of the Birmingham and Stafford Chronicle:

Gentlemen, the information you gave in your last paper, of one thousand families in the town of Birmingham having left off the use of sugar, with a view to forward the abolition of the slave trade, must be a pleasing reflection to every humane mind. Many families, Sir, in the town of Walsall, have adopted similar resolutions to the same motives.

The lines subjoined, were occasioned by seeing two young gentlemen, who are brothers, denying themselves the pleasing and fashionable repast of Tea, from a like resolution never to taste sugar more till produced by free men. I will thank you to publish them in your next Chronicle, the importance and the novelty of the subject, it is presumed, will preponderate against any imperfection in the composition.

I am gentlemen, your humble servant

H. Walsall.

Most worthy youths! Of resolution rare,
Tea to forgo and sugar to forbear,
Because the cane, the luscious luxury rear'd
By human slaves, whipt till with blood besmeared.
The cruelties and anguish, pain and woe
Which negro-slaves (poor wretches!) undergo.
One of yourselves has seen, and thence deny,
The produce of such misery to enjoy.
Prise-worthy conduct! Motive so refined
Displays a feeling and exalted mind.

Birmingham and Staffordshire Chronicle,
c. January 1792 (v.3, p.38)

~

RANELAGH

On Monday, the seventh of May, will be displayed in Ranelagh Garden a capital FIREWORK, in honour of the birth-day of her royal highness the Duchess of York. After which a most Magnificent and Grand representation of the Eruption and Flowing of the lava of Mount Ætna, on a scale much larger than ever exhibited.

Under the Mountain will be shown the cavern of Vulcan, with the Cyclops at work forging the armour of Mars, as described in the Æneid of Virgil.

The music complied from Gluck, Hayden, Giardini and Handel.

The Building and Painting of the mountain designed and executed by Seignior Gaetano Marinari, Painter to the opera.

The scene represents a cavern, on one side of which is adorned with ancient arms and instruments of war; and on the other side is seen a forge, near which the Cyclops are stretched fast asleep. Vulcan appears, and (exasperated to find his Works neglected) commands them to return to their labour. Presently Venus and Cupid visit him; the former to request arms for Æneas, the latter to beg he would temper his arrows. Next Mars arrives, petitioning for armour, who seeing Venus, pays court to her. Whereupon Vulcan concealing his inquietude, shews the spectators the curious net he had ingeniously contrived to entrap them, if they should be found together, and presents Mars with a suit of armour, the workmanship of which he greatly admires. Mars, Venus and Cupid retiring, Vulcan and the Cyclops commence their operations. – The smoke thickens, the crater on the top of Ætna vomits forth flames, and the lava rolls dreadful along the side of the mountain. This continues with increasing violence, till there is a prodigious eruption, which finishes with a tremendous explosion.

Admittance five S. Coffee and tea included.

The Star, Thursday 26 April 1792 (v.2, p.145)

To the editor of Lloyd's Evening Post:
Sir,
The Present price of provisions in general is very

alarming, and if not remedied by those who have it in their power, may be attended with the most dangerous consequences. It is hereby recommended to the ministry and both Houses of Parliament, to lay a tax on all sorts of dogs, of 5s annually, kept by the Nobility, Gentry, Yeomanry, Farmers, Labourers & etc. In that part of Great Britain called England, the principality of Wales, and the town of Berwick upon Tweed. And it is hoped that no person, either rich or poor, will be offended, when they consider the matter as the writer intends it, his motive being to do good.

To begin with London. Every person who knows it is sensible of there being too many dogs kept, as they are seldom wanted but where the Tradesman's property is out of doors, and they are few in proportion. Ladies and Gentlemen who keep lap dogs by way of diversion, and keep them better than many poor families live, cannot refuse so small a sum for the sake of their petty play-things, and if they would rather destroy them than pay so small a tax, their servants may be employed to much better services, and more to their own satisfaction.

The number of dogs is calculated to be near one million, and if by this means 500,000 could be knocked on the head, the remaining moiety will produce 125,000l. sterling annually, and it is computed at a very moderate calculation there are annually destroyed by canine species near 200,000 sheep and lambs, which, suppose on average worth 10s., amounts to no less a sum than 100,000l. sterling; this, with the consumption of those who are well fed in houses, kennels & etc. will soon produce a considerable balance; and after all, what dreadful consequences happen to many by being bit when these poor animals run mad, a thought worthy of the consideration of the wisest and best of men.

Rusticus Londinenis.

[NOTE: A dog tax was eventually levied on all 'working dogs with tails', between 1796 and 1847. The aim of the tax was to assist the government in gathering revenue, as well as (by lowering the number of dogs in total) to reduce attacks on livestock and people. Fewer dogs would also ease the pressure on provisions, and reduce the risk of bouts of hydrophobia (rabies). The tax led to a change in pet fashion; creating a trend for dogs with docked tails.]

Lloyd's Evening Post, c. **January 1771 (v.3, p.91)**

~

STAGE EFFECT!

A translation from our play of HAMLET has been got up in Holland, and, being considerably *enlarged* and *aukwardized*, is affirmed by the Dutch to be much better than the original.

But the improvement of which they are most proud is the *stage effect* of the Ghost scene. There the start and stare of the actor are assisted by a contrivance never to be surpassed, consisting in the insertion of a small invisible spring under HAMLET'S wig, a thread communicating with which falls behind the actor's ear. When the Ghost is upon the point of appearing, the actor, unseen or unnoticed, touches the thread behind his *off* ear, and as the *Ghost enters*, off flies his *wig!*

A sub-wig then appears, in which bristles painted and stiffened, are wrought into the appearance of locks; and thus the *Dutch* say they fulfil the intention of the Ghost, by making

Each particular hair to stand on end,
Like quills upon the fretful porcupine.

[NOTE: Esteemed actor David Garrick (1717–79) played his first Hamlet in Dublin in 1742, and his last (in what was his final performance) in 1776. Towards the end of his career, a wig-maker and hairdresser called Perkins constructed for Garrick a mechanical wig, the bristles of which indeed rose, accentuating the aspect of fear. Whilst not quite as flamboyant as the Dutch flip-wig, which was to come later, it was perhaps significantly less awkward on the eye.]

Gazetteer and New Daily Advertiser, c. **November 1792 (v.3, p.97)**

~

MAGICAL INCANTATION

A farmer at Aldenham, near Watford, in Hertfordshire, who a few weeks since had observed some unusual symptoms in a mare, which eluded the skill of the farrier, was advised by his neighbours to have her shot; but so it happened, that no sooner was the fatal tube got ready, than the animal appeared perfectly well, and another mare was seized with the disorder, in reality nothing more than the staggers. – This sudden transition was immediately deemed *witchcraft* by the farmer's wife, and some of her companions; which had such an effect upon the good man, that he was easily persuaded to procure some of its urine, and to mix it with a number of crooked pins, which being close corked up in a bottle, was to be set on the fire till the supposed witch should come to the house! These directions were strictly attended to, but on the increase of the heat, the vessel not only burst with a loud explosion, but some of the pieces were so forcibly driven into the faces of the observers, that they have not yet been able to appear in public, without undergoing the laugh of the village; yet, what tends the more to confirm them in their superstition is, that neither of the horses have had a single fit since the ceremony was performed.

[NOTE: After 1735 the act of witchcraft was no longer a crime, though fortune tellers and the like had begun to be prosecuted as fraudsters. Despite this, lingering convictions persisted in more rural areas.]

Public Advertiser, **Thursday 31 May 1792 (v.3, p.98)**

At Miranda del Ebro a parrot and monkey were lately convicted of heresy and blasphemy, and sentenced to be burnt. The parrot for repeating – *To the Devil with the Roman Magpye, and a fig for the Pope* – and the monkey for seeming to applaud, by grinning and chattering, and dancing. The sentence was publicly executed with all the solemnity used

in burning heretics, to the great edification of the
devout Spaniards.

Evening Mail, **Wednesday 12 October 1791**
(v.3, p.100)

DOCTOR'S COMMONS
SATURDAY, NOV. 9.
DIVORCE
MORSON *versus* MORSON

This was a suit instituted by the Plaintiff against his Wife, to obtain a Divorce *a menia et thoro*, for adultery with a Mr. CLARK.

It appeared the parties lived at Whitby and had carried on a criminal intercourse for a considerable time. – The Plaintiff brought an Action for *Crim. Con.* against Mr. CLARK, and obtained a verdict for 3,500l.

The Wife set up a plea, in which she stated, that her Husband had been guilty of the most gross contrivance, inasmuch as several persons at Whitby had particularly observed the great intimacy that subsisted between Mr. CLARK and Mrs. MORSON, and which was not taken notice of by Mr. MORSON. – The familiarities that remained unnoticed by the Husband, and that the Counsel for Mrs. MORSON particularly dwelt upon, were, that Mr. CLARK frequently visited Mrs. MORSON; that the parties sat before the Husband with Mrs.

MORSON's hand in Mr. CLARK's; that Mr. CLARK made the lady several presents; that the Husband was in the habit of leaving the parties alone; that Mr. CLARK frequently drove Mrs. MORSON out to take the air; and that on a remonstrance made by the Lady's Mother concerning this intimacy, to Mr. MORSON, in which she said 'that if no other mischief would be done, her Daughter's character would at least be ruined,' he replied, 'that his best customer must on no account be affronted,' – for it seems Mr. CLARK was in the habit of buying timber from the Plaintiff.

Public Advertiser, **Friday 15 November 1793 (v.3, p.181)**

POOLE, NOV, 17.

An accident of a serious nature happened at St. John's in Newfoundland, on board of His Majesty's ship the *Stately*. – The Captain having ordered one of the Gunner's Mates to be punished for neglect of duty, it was of course put into execution; but it so much hurt the pride of the man, that from thence he was determined to take the life of the Captain.

A few days after, he with some others were sent into the magazine to do some necessary business; after the work was done the rest of his companions could not get him out of the place where they had been employed. He told them he never would leave it until the Captain came and spoke to him; this the Captain very prudently refused to do; but in order to induce him to come out, the Gunner personated him – the man told him to put his head down and speak to him, which he did; and he really supposing it to be the Captain, instantly fired off a pistol, which shot the unfortunate Gunner through the head, and he expired immediately.

The Ship's Crew hearing an explosion in the Magazine, naturally supposed that it had blown up, and there were about one hundred men instantly leaped over-board, and unfortunately eight of them are drowned.

Morning Post, **Wednesday 20 November 1793**
(v.3, p.185)

~

AN ACCOUNT OF A

MACCARONI

In Italy, but particularly in Naples they make a kind of composition called *Maccaroni*, which is a considerable part of the food of the people, and is always a dish at every table in one shape in another. It is nothing else but flour and water wrought into a paste; which paste is either put into long moulds, with a rod in the middle of them, by which means they are cast of forms as pipes or reeds or paste, the composition is dried to a very moderate degree, and then it is fit to be used in the kitchen. The intention of making it hollow is that it may boil the sooner. After it is boiled, and all the water is drained from it, the taste of it is worse than insipid; for any taste it has is a kind of greasy taste, like tallow or soap. It is therefore put into meat or gravy soup, or mixed up with butter and cheese.

c. **December 1771 (v.3, p.200)**

INSANITY

Private mad-houses are becoming so general at present, and their prostitution of justice so openly carried, that any man may have his wife, his father, or his brother, confined for life at a certain stipulated price! The wretched victims are concealed from the inspecting Doctors, unless it can be contrived, that they shall be stupefied with certain drugs, or made mad with strong liquors against the hours of visiting! – There should be no such receptacle as a private mad-house allowed, and the relations and friends of the insane should be allowed to visit at all times.

(v.4, p.8)

SIR,

In Governor Thicknesse's Gentleman's Guide in his Tour round through France is the following passage in his account of Rouen in Normandy: 'There are three small rivers which run through the town; one of which is much frequented by frogs, though one would imagine that in time they would be destroyed, as they commonly compose a dish or two at each meal at the tables of both rich and poor; the latter mostly living on them.'

On reading this passage it occurred to me, that if our poor would conquer the prejudice of education, they might (at this time especially, when the price of every kind of provision is extravagantly dear) procure frogs as food for themselves and families gratis, as most of the Ponds and Ditches in England are filled with them.

A French Gentleman tells me, that when cut, washed and fryed with Butter, Parsley, &c. they form a dish, which, were you not told to the contrary, you would suppose a fricassee of chickens. It may be objected that the ignorant may gather toads with their frogs. I answer, they cannot be deceived when they are once informed of the difference: The colour of the frog is a light brown, the toad is almost black; the frog always leaps, the toad creeps.

The Writer of this letter recommends not this dish as food for every Englishman; no, let those who have it in their power, sit down every day to roast beef; but as he is convinced there are very great numbers of our poor at this time starving, he throws out this hint for their benefit.

A FRIEND to the POOR.

Public Advertiser, **Saturday 23 May 1772**
(v.4, p.100)

~

A CARD

A number of Officers, lately promoted in the Land and Sea Service, beg leave to present their compliments to *Don Francisco Bucearelli*, and return him their most grateful acknowledgements for his spirited behaviour in taking Falkland's Isle, being conscious, that, had it not been through him,

they must have remained many years unnoticed.
Feb. 25. 1771. CORPORAL TRIM

> [NOTE: Sovereignty over the islands has long
> been contested, though the Falkland Crisis of
> 1770 (alluded to above) was the first time factions
> approached a full-scale war over the territories.]

c. February 1771 (v.4, p.144)

A fellow at Windsor, who lately ate a cat, has given
another proof of the brutality of his disposition –
an instance too ferocious and sanguinary, almost,
to admit of public representation.

He was at a public-house at Old Windsor, one day
in the course of last week, and, without apparent
cause, walked out of the house, and with a bill-hook
severed his hand from his arm. His brutal courage
was strongly marked in this transformation; for
the inhuman monster made three strokes with the
instrument before he could effect his purpose, and
at last actually made a complete amputation. He
assigns no other reason for this terrible self-attack

than his total disinclination to work, and that this step will compel the overseers of his parish to provide for him during the remainder of his life.

General Evening Post, Saturday 30 January 1790
(v5, p.115)

~

AN APPROVED METHOD OF

DESTROYING WEOVILS

The smell of lobsters is fatal to those voracious insects; lobsters have been thrown alive among wheat infected with weovils, and in a short time the walls of the barn were covered with them; if the lobsters be left till they become putrid, the insects will all die, and the corn be entirely cleared of them.

(v.5, p.148)

A few days since, while Mr. Brogdon, of Waltham-Abbey, was angling with trolling tackle in the River Lea, near that town, his bait, which was a live gudgeon was gorged by an Otter, which was brought to land; but by a sudden spring, he got off with about fifty yards of spun silk line, and part of the fishing rod.

The Sun, **Thursday 25 April 1793 (v.8, p.74)**

Last Tuesday a new trick was played upon the public: – A Man with a monkey on his shoulders was standing before Somerset-house, which gathered a number of people together. A Lady passing by at the same time, the monkey leapt upon her shoulder, which alarmed her much; but two well looking men flew to her assistance, who, by hugging her close, and taking the Monkey off, found means to carry off her purse, and thirty guineas.

The Sun, **Tuesday 30 April 1793 (v.8, p.94)**

A pitched battle was lately fought at Elmstead, in the neighbourhood of Chelmsford, by two women; being stripped, without caps, and their hair tied close, to it they set, and for forty-five minutes maintained a most desperate conflict: one of them, an adept in the science, beat her antagonist in a most shocking manner, and would most probably have killed her, but for the interference of the spectators. To the vanquished heroine her husband was bottle-holder, and with a degree of barbarity that would have disgraced a savage, we are informed he instigated his fair rib to the fight.

The Star, Monday 22 July 1793 (v.8, p.250)

On Monday last was picked near Aston Park Wall, a mushroom that measured round the head 3 feet 9 inches, the stem 6 inches, weighed three pounds and a half, and when baked, produced a quart of catchup.

The Sun, Thursday 17 October 1793 (v.9, p.134)

Female loquacity has ever been a subject for wit to shoot arrows at: how unjustly so those who have the happiness of much frequenting female society in the present age will readily testify. A Capuchin Friar, however, of a contrary opinion, preaching before the inhabitants of a Nunnery, having said many fine things of Mary Magdalen, added, 'But do not, my beloved, be too proud that our blessed lord paid your sex the distinguishing honour of appearing first to a female after his resurrection; for it was done that the glad tidings might spread the sooner.'

Courier and *Evening Gazette*, Saturday
19 December 1795 (v.9, p.1)

Thomas Bruce was indicted for breaking and entering the dwelling house of ALEXANDER MITCHEL, privately in the night time, and stealing therein various articles of wearing apparel, and two guineas, on the 5th of this month, the property of ALEXANDER MITCHEL.

The evidence being satisfactory, the Jury found the prisoner – *Guilty, Death.* – But on account of his youth, being only 17, he was recommended to mercy, of which the proper officer was directed by Mr. Justice Rook to make a note.

Joseph Chapman was found guilty on an indictment for burglariously breaking and entering the dwelling house of EDWARD WARNER, or Paradise-row, Chelsea, Cheesemonger, and stealing therein, on the 19th of December last, about 8 o'clock at night, a cheese of 64 pounds weight. – *Death.*

The Morning Chronicle, Thursday 16 January 1794 (v.10, p.59)

~

THE NATIONAL DEBT

On the fifth of January, 1784, was stated at the enormous sum of TWO HUNDRED AND SEVENTY-TWO MILLIONS Sterling. This, according to DR. PRICE, would, if laid down in guineas, form a line extending more than 4,300 miles; in shillings, three and a half times round the world; and if in solid silver, would require 60,400 horses to draw it, allowing 1500lb weight to each horse.

World, **Tuesday 7 January 1794 (v.10, p.84)**

The church-yards of Lambeth, St. John's, Westminster, Whitechapel and Hampstead have lately been plundered of their dead. In a house lately demolished near Whitechapel, as the receptacle of stolen bodies, the mysteries of this detestable traffic were found out; – that they were boiled in large coopers – the fat was skimmed off for the candle makers – the flesh disposed of for dog's meat, and feeding wild beasts – and the bones of course disposed of to the surgeons as usual; so that these dealers in human flesh now make, upon an average, five guineas of every corpse they plunder from its grave.

London Packet or *Lloyd's Evening Post*, **Monday 24 March 1794 (v.10, p.186)**

~

COVENT GARDEN THEATRE

THE SPEECHLESS

WIFE – FARCE

Rumour gives this piece to a Lady of Fashion. As it has totally failed, we shall give her the advantage of concealment. The Music filled us with astonishment – any thing so detestably dull, without contrivance, or even decent plagiarism, we never heard before.

c. **1794 (v.11, p.1)**

FASHION

The feminine dress of the present period is, perhaps, the most indecent ever worn in this country – the breast is altogether displayed; and the whole drapery, by the wanton management of the wearer, in throwing it behind her, is made to cling close to the figure, that nothing can be said to be completely concealed. Well may it be necessary to veil the face!

London Packet or Lloyd's Evening Post, **Monday 30 June 1794 (v.11, p.74)**

On Monday James Roach, Bookseller, was called up to receive the judgement of the court of King's Bench, for having published an infamous pamphlet, entitled Harris's list of Covent Garden ladies.

Mr. Justice Ashhurst observed, that an offence of greater enormity could hardly be committed. A care of the growing morals of the present generation ought to be uppermost in every man's heart. The only circumstance of mitigation in the present case was that the defendant had had the decency to let judgement go by default. It had been stated that the defendant was a married man, and had a wife and six children. That circumstance ought to have been considered by him before committing the offence. The court ordered that the defendant should be imprisoned in his Majesty's jail of Newgate for twelve calendar months.

[NOTE: As this short report suggests, the bookseller, James (or John) Roach, had a rather novel approach to selling books. His bookshop on Drury Lane stocked everything from children's anthologies to salacious prints, and he is credited with producing one of the first part-publications – a collection of poetry published over two years. Selling *Harris's List* (a notorious catalogue of courtesans and their various specialisms) was a step too far, landing him with a full year's incarceration. However, the consummate entrepreneur, Roach managed to turn this to his own ends, and with his newfound

notoriety released a selection of theatre books
that sold rather well.]

**London Packet or New Lloyd's Evening Post,
Thursday 29 January 1795 (v.11, p.108)**

∽

JAMES BOSWELL

This gentleman who died on Tuesday last, has
made such a distinguished figure in the Literary
World, that he should not be suffered to drop into
the grave without notice.

His original powers of mind were not of the
higher kind, but they were greater than has been
generally supposed. He possessed humour, and
was not without learning. If he had cultivated his
poetical talents, he would most probably have
acquired no inconsiderable repute in the sportive
province. His darling propensity was an avarice of
Fame; and this propensity he indulged rather by
courting the acquaintance of celebrated characters,

than by drawing from the resources of his own mind.

He made his entrance into public life by an account of the famous Pascal Paoli, and by the extravagant zeal which marked his representation of the Corsican hero, Mr. Boswell contrived to elevate himself. When he had sufficiently exalted the character of Paoli for the purposes of deriving a reflected fame for himself, he found means to get into particular intimacy with Dr. Johnson, and of course became known to all the literary connections of the great British Moralist. By his intercession Johnson was induced to gratify an early desire of visiting the Western Islands of Scotland, and Mr. Boswell had the pleasure of being the *Cicerone* to the literary *Leviathon*, and of *shewing him about* to all *curious people* of the North.

Of this expedition Boswell wrote an account, and in his History of Sam. Johnson's Rambles, he did not forget to take due notice of himself.

The Sun, Saturday 23 May 1795 (v.11, p.178)

Just as this paper was putting to Press, we received, by EXPRESS, the Paris *Journals* of the 26th and 27th inst. The intelligence they contain is extremely important, but the lateness of the hour precludes the possibility of giving anything more than a mere outline in this day's Paper.

The accounts brought by the Vessel that arrived from Calais mention that Paris is in a state of extreme confusion and disorder. – In the tumults that appear to have taken place several lives are stated to have been lost; and the Convention, seeing the determined resolution of the Sections to oppose the attempts for perpetuating their power, are preparing to quit the Metropolis.

CIVIL WAR IN PARIS
The contents of the papers which we have received, warrant us in saying, *that a civil war has actually broke out in Paris!!*

c. September 1795 (v.12, p.61)

All the vaults in the churches have been opened and their leaded coffins taken up, to be cut into balls. The people have signified their intention of purchasing from the town of St. Dennis the lead of all the coffins of the Abbey Church there (the burying place, for many ages of the Kings of France) in case the inhabitants should be otherwise sufficiently provided with ball.

[NOTE: The Monastery of Saint-Denis (burial ground for nearly every king of France) suffered severe damage during the French Revolution due to its proximity to Paris and links with the monarchy. Not only were tombs desecrated to provide shot, but also the treasury was melted and the roof torn off. The building was transformed into a Temple of Reason.]

c. **September 1795 (v.6)**

October 14

The seals are still fixed upon the presses of several Journalists. Some of them are imprisoned, and their papers are stopped. A warrant was issued for the apprehension of SUARD one of the editors of the *Nouvelles Politiques*, for having represented the late events at Paris in an unfavourable point of view – but he made his escape.

***St James's Chronicle or the British Evening Post*, Tuesday 20 October 1795 (v.12, p.113)**

~

BRIGHTON, *SEPT. 29*

A curious circumstance occurred at Brighton on Monday. – Sir John Lade, for a trifling wager, undertook to carry Lord Cholmondely *on his back*, from opposite the Pavilion twice round the Steine. Several Ladies attended to be spectators of this extraordinary feat of the dwarf carrying a giant. When his lordship declared himself ready, Sir John desired he should *strip*. 'Strip!' exclaimed the other; 'why, surely, you promised to carry me in my clothes!' – 'By no means,' replied the Baronet; 'I engaged to carry *you*, but not an inch of clothes. – So therefore, my Lord, make ready, and let us not *disappoint* the Ladies.' After much laughable altercation, it was decided at length that Sir John had won his wager, the peer declining to exhibit *in puris naturalibus*.

[NOTE: Sir John Lade was well known from an early age to Samuel Johnson, who apparently was underwhelmed by the intelligence of the former.

Dr Johnson contributed the following lines on the occasion of Sir John's twenty-first birthday – the age at which he inherited a fortune:

Long-expected one-and-twenty
Ling'ring year, at length is flown
Pride and pleasure, pomp and plenty
Great Sir John, are now your own.

Loosen'd from the minor's tether,
Free to mortgage or to sell.
Wild as wind, and light as feather
Bid the sons of thrift farewell

Johnson's lines were an accurate prognostication. Lade's obsession with horses (he appeared in riding attire with a whip at all times) and betting (such fabulous wagers as the above) landed him in arrears. To avoid the debtor's prison he took a pension, and the title of driving tutor to King George.]

***Oracle and Public Advertiser*, Thursday 1 October 1795 (v.12, p.67)**

Mr. Brown, one of the superintendants of the gardens of Lady Heathcote, at North End, near Hammersmith, amusing himself with flying an electrical kite near a thunder cloud, by some unfortunate mismanagement of apparatus, had neglected the proper precautions requisite for conveying the electrical fluid to the earth, when, on a sudden, the cloud burst with a most tremendous shock, and Mr. Brown, with the horse he rode on, was struck with instant death. Mr. Brown has left a wife and five children to mourn his untimely loss. – The Jury have already sat on the body of Mr. Brown and brought in a verdict of accidental death.

Courier and Evening Gazette, **Wednesday 28 October 1795 (v.12, p.75)**

~

PARTICULARS RESPECTING

WOLD COTTAGE

PHÆNOMENON

In a letter from Mr Topham to a Friend:
The singular phænomenon which took place near my house in Yorkshire on Sunday 20th of December, 1795, has excited general curiosity. For a space of three weeks thirty or forty persons on each day had come to see the stone that had fallen; and I found likewise a number of letters from different parts of the kingdom, requesting me to give them an account of the circumstance.

The following detail, which you are welcome to make public, will be, I hope satisfactory on the subject:- The exact weight of the stone which fell, and which was weighed immediately on being dug up, was, by Merlin's balance, 3 stone, 13 pounds. On being measured it had buried itself in 12 inches of soil, after that in six inches of solid chalk rock, from whence it was some little time in being extracted. When taken up it was warm and smoaked. At the time it fell there was a labourer within nine yards and a carpenter and joiner of mine within seventy yards. The labourer saw it coming down, at the distance of ten yards from the ground. As it fell, a number of explosions were heard by the three men, at short intervals, about as loud as the report of a pistol. The stone is strongly impregnated with sulphur, and then smelt very strongly. The general texture of the stone is of grey granite, of which I know of none that can be called 'natives of this country'. What renders this event the more extraordinary is, that the day was mild and hazy; a sort of weather very frequent on the Wold Hills, when there are no winds or storms: but there was not any thunder or lightening the whole day.

From all the various persons who have been to inspect this curiosity, and who are still coming daily from different parts, no satisfactory conjecture has yet been hazarded from whence it can have come. We have no such stone in the country. There has not been any where in these parts an eruption from the earth. From its jagged and irregular form, it cannot have come from any building; and as the day was not tempestuous, it does not seem probable that it can have been forced from any works, the nearest of which are those of Flamborough-head, a distance of twelve miles. The particulars of the event are now before the public. I have taken every due care to examine the accounts given by different persons, who all agree to the subject; and from what I have seen I have no doubts about the veracity of their relation. To account for the extraordinary appearance, I leave to the researches of the philosopher,

It's have the honour to be,

  Sir,

    Your humble servant

      Edward Topham

[NOTE: This meteorite was the first recorded fall observed in Britain, and is (at 25kg) the second largest to be found. 'Topham's Stone' and the account of its arrival were key pieces of evidence, confirming that meteors were indeed stones from the firmament, and that though matter existed beyond the earth, it was in many ways alike. Topham was mindful that, whilst astronomically significant, the stone possessed a material value.

He took it ontour to a Piccadilly coffee shop, where a shilling bought a view, as well as an exact engraving of the stone. Over time the stone was broken up and distributed, and fragments are still on show at the Natural History Museum, London.]

Oracle and Public Advertiser, Friday 12 February 1796 (v.12, p.183)

~

CRICKET MATCH

Yesterday, from the novelty of an advertisement announcing a Cricket Match to be played by eleven Greenwich pensioners with *one leg* against eleven with *one arm*, for one thousand guineas, at the new Cricket ground, Montpelier Gardens, Walworth, an immense concourse of people assembled. About nine o'clock the men arrived in three Greenwich stages; about ten the wickets were pitched, and the match commenced. Those with but one leg had the first innings, and got 93 runs. At about three o'clock, while those with but one arm were having their innings, a scene of riot and confusion took place, owing to the pressure of the populace to gain admittance to the ground; the gates were forced open, and several parts of the fencing were broke down, and a great number of persons having got upon the roof of a stable, the roof broke in, and several of them falling among the horses, were taken out much bruised. About six o'clock the game was renewed, and those with but one arm got but 42 runs during their innings. The one legs commenced their second innings, and six were bowled out after they got 60, so that they left off 111 more than those with one arm.

[NOTE: Cricket matches pitting monopods against one-armed teams were more common than one might perhaps expect. As noted above, the events attracted huge crowds and were an ideal means of collecting money for the disabled players. In this case, the benefactors were the Greenwich Pensioners – the naval equivalent of the Chelsea Pensioners. Apparently it was usual for the team with only one leg to emerge victorious, though in 1841, when the Greenwich Pensioners took on the

Chelsea Pensioners, the former won by 176 runs to
19 – despite having more one-legged players.]

The Sun, Wednesday 10 August 1796 (v.12, p.224)

*Recipe to keep a person warm the whole winter with
a single Billet of Wood.* – Take a billet of wood the
ordinary size, run up into the garret with it as quick
as you can, throw it out of the garret window; run
down after it (not out of the garret window mind)
as fast as possible; repeat this till *you are warm*, and
as often as occasion may require. It will never fail
to have the desired effect whilst you are able to use
it. – *Probatum est.*

**Oracle and Public Advertiser, Thursday
24 November 1796 (v.12, p.253)**

~

EXHIBITION

Mrs. Bullock presents her most respectful
compliments to the Ladies and Gentlemen of
Birmingham and its Vicinity, and begs leave to
inform them, that she is just arrived with a most
beautiful Cabinet of WAX FIGURES, which are not
busts, but the full Size of Life, striking Likenesses
of the Persons they represent, and are dressed in
the most fashionable and splendid Manner of their
respective countries. – The Figures are principally
as follow: The King and Queen of England, the
Prince and Princess of Wales, the Duke and
Duchess of York, and Princes Royal. The King,
Prince of Wales, and Duke of York are dressed in
uniforms that have been worn by themselves. The
unfortunate Royal Family of France, consisting
of the late King, Queen, Dauphin, and Madame
Elizabeth, sister to the King, and Princes Royal.
This group was done from original Models
taken at Paris in the beginning of the late Events
by the celebrated Monsieur Oudon, sculptor to

Louis XVI, and a member of the Royal academy. A very capital representation of a Tippoo Sultan, and his two Sons, who were given as Hostages to the Marquis Cornwallis, in the East-Indies. This figure of Tippoo, which stands upwards of six feet high, is universally allowed to be the most expressive and lively figure that ever was executed in England. Catherine empress of Russia … Ussuff Aguiah Effendi, the Turkish ambassador, done from life … The Hon. Charles James Fox. The Hon. William Pitt, late Earl of Chatham, an Impression from his own face. A fine figure of the late Dr. Franklyn, of America. A Figure of one of his majesties Yeomen of the Guards, in his full uniform. An old Politician. A Nurse and child. A party at a Card Table.

The whole of this valuable Cabinet of Elegant and Interesting Figures, which forms a rational Exhibition, equally gratifying to the ingenious artist and the curious inspector, is now open for public inspection at a House No. 29, near the Bank, Bull-street from Ten in the Morning, till Nine at Night.

Admittance, One Shilling. Servants and children Half Price. Tickets of Admission may be had at the place of exhibition.

The company are desired not to bring dogs.

[NOTE: Towards the end of the eighteenth century, collections of wax figures were to become an increasingly popular form of entertainment. It was a direct result of the troubles in France that Madame Tussaud (one-time art tutor to the sister of King Louis XVI) emigrated to England where her exhibition was to become a fixture on Baker Street. In a world devoid of glossy magazines, the wax figure was one means of marketing celebrity and bringing news from abroad to life. Trade and newspapers had widened the horizons of many, engendering a natural interest in the appearance of visitors from foreign lands. The wax statues, at full size, in full costume, and (most importantly) in full colour, would have been more engaging than any engraving. The entreaty not to bring dogs needs no explanation.]

(v.12, p.255)

CAUTION – Lately died at Dundsdon Green, Oxon; after twelve days painful illness, Mr. C. Langford, formerly an eminent farmer and grazier of that place. His death was occasioned by eating a large quantity of cherries, and very imprudently swallowing the stones, which produced an obstruction in his bowels, terminating in a mortification. Thus fell a hearty hale constitution, a woeful sacrifice to the incautious use of fruit.

London Packet or New Lloyd's Evening Post,
Wednesday 7 September 1796 (v.12, p.277)

The PLUM PUDDING EATER, after eight days gormandizing, was necessitated to *give in!* He was to have eaten a square foot, 42 lbs. in a fortnight.

The Telegraph, **Wednesday 11 January 1799**
(v.12, p.289)

~

BOTANY-BAY THEATRICALS

The following is a copy of the Play-Bill just arrived from Botany-Bay; for there, it seems, Plays are now performed by the Convicts:

By Permission of his Excellency.
For the benefit of H. Green
On Saturday, July 23, 1796, will be performed,
THE BUSY BODY.
Marplot, W. Fokes;
Sir Francis Gripe, L. Jones;
Charles, W. Chapmen;
Sir Jealous Traffic, H Green; Whisper, R Evans;
And Sir George Airy, J. Sparrow.
Isabina, Mrs. Greville; Patch, Mrs. Radley;
And Miranda, Mrs. Davis.

With THE POOR SOLDIER.
Patrick H. Lavell;
Fitzroy, R. Mumby; Father Luke, H. Green;

Dermot, R. Evans; Darby, W. Fokes;
Kathleen, H. Wynn;
And Norah, Mrs. Greville.

Front Boxes, 3s. 6d. Pit, 2s. 6d. Gallery 1s.

H. Green was transported for picking pockets. Mrs. Radley was convicted of perjury, in attempting to screen her husband in a trial for robbery.

Sidway was transported for returning twice from transportation; he was one of the first that went out to Botany-Bay, transported for a burglary, and was appointed baker to the Colony, in which situation he has realised 3000l. His time for transportation has been long expired, but he does not chuse to leave the Settlement, where he has a great prospect of increasing his wealth.

Morning Post and *Fashionable World*,
Thursday 13 July 1797 (v.13, p.22)

The plays at *Botany Bay*, it has been observed, are all cast with much strength. How can it otherwise be considered, when it is recollected that the *Dramatis Personaæ* consists of well known *tried performers* who have long boasted much *ability* in *their line*. We need not add, that the audience are completely *transported*.

[NOTE: Botany Bay, in Sydney, New South Wales, was the site of Cook's first landfall in Australia. Between 1788 and 1868 the Bay became a destination for British convicts who had committed crimes not serious enough to warrant hanging, but too serious to be punished by a fine. Reports and recorded folk culture suggest that life on board the ships and at the penal colony could be abysmal; however, this was not enough to prevent Australia's first theatre opening in 1796.]

***Morning Herald*, Saturday 22 July 1797 (v.13, p.42)**

~

DIED

On the 1st instant at Whitby, in the 97th year of his age, Mr. Thomas Brignell, an eminent Whitesmith and ingenious mechanic: his name has long been known in most of the ports of England, particularly in those trading to the Baltic and Greenland seas, for the excellence of his screws and harpoons. Long before the birth of Mr. Moore, of Cheapside, he in conjunction with a Mr. Wilson, a brother schemer of the same place, formed a carriage to travel without horses. This, after being admired for a time, was at last neglected; like most inventions where utility is not the offspring of ingenuity.

c. **February 1797 (v.13, p.88)**

~

ARTS AND SCIENCES

PHYSIOLOGY

Spallanzani, having destroyed the eyes of bats and set them at liberty in an apartment, observed that they could guide themselves from one place to another as before. They avoided every object that was presented to them, and even passed through rings which were placed before them, and for this reason he asks, 'May not these animals possess a sense with which we are not acquainted, and which may supply that of sight; or, may not smell be sufficient for that purpose?'

Jurine is of the opinion that it is hearing which supplies the above want. He filled with wax one of the ears of those animals which he had deprived of sight, and he observed that they flew about with difficulty: when he filled both their ears they could not fly at all.

c. August 1798 (v.13, p.250)

COMMON PLEAS – Yesterday Barton, an attorney, was brought from the Fleet prison. It was stated that the prisoner had written a very violent and voluminous libel on *himself*. This he procured to be printed, and then brought his action against the printer for defamation; but in this he was non-suited, and sent to prison for costs attending to the prosecution.

Observer, Sunday 11 November 1798 (v.13, p.289)

Hoaxing has been all the fashion this summer at Brighton; and there was never a better hoax played off than the following: - Some laughter-loving Bucks sent a love-letter to a certain *Baronet*, from a *Tooth-drawer's* wife. The baronet went to her house, and there meeting her husband, he was compelled to say he had a *tooth-ache*, and actually submitted to having one *bone* taken out, in order to save the rest from being broken.

The Star, Friday 30 November 1798 (v.13, p.229)

~

EPIGRAM

On the newly imported Female Mode of wearing Watches at the Bosum:

Among our fashionable bands,
No wonder, now, if *Time* should linger;
Allow'd to place his *two* rude *hands*
Where others dare not lay a finger.

(v.14, p.161)

The *skipping-rope, tambourine,* and even the marrial *cymbol,* are all giving way to the more feminine delights of *foot-ball*; a sportive instrument now kicking about the most fashionable drawing-rooms for a morning exercise! The *Gallic Dancing-master* recommends it as the best introductionto the *Amazonian* grace, and the admiring mothers adopt the measure, in the fond hope, that it may tend to

keep their daughter-hood in future more firmly on their legs!

Morning Herald, Friday 11 July 1800 (v.14, p.169)

MATRIMONY. – It is much to be regretted, but indisputably certain, that many persons of both sexes are deterred from entering into the married state by secret infirmities, which delicacy forbids them to disclose; and there are not a few who, being already married, are rendered miserable for want of those tender pledges of mutual love, without which happiness this state is at least very precarious. It has been ascertained beyond a doubt, that those circumstances are occasioned by general or partial relaxation or weakening in either sex, and it is equally certain that the genuine AROMATIC LOZENGES OF STEEL, are the best, if not the only remedy ever discovered for this species of disability. When taken into the stomach, they immediately dissolve and diffuse like a vapour through every pore, producing effects at once delightful, salutary and permanent. When the spark of life begins to grow dim, the circulation languid, and the faculties paralyzed, these Lozenges are found to give tone to the nerves, exhilarate the animal spirits, invigorate the body, and reanimate the whole man.

Oracle and Daily Advertiser, Wednesday 24 September 1800 (v.14, p.261)

~

FOR THE RUPTURED,

CROOKED, LAME AND

DEFORMED

J. Edy, No. 43, Dean-street Soho, recommends to the notice of those afflicted with every kind of Ruptures his PATENT ELASTIC TRUSSES, as being superior to any ever made, never failing the desired effect, in relieving and curing Ruptures of every sort. Likewise his Concave Bandages for corpulent persons, and Naval Ruptures, the best ever invented, – those Trusses have one, two, three and four different motions of elasticity, according to the nature of the case, and the state of the complaint, conveniently adapted for men, women and children. Trusses mended, covered and improved. – Bag Trusses, to preserve in riding with tumours. He also makes every other sort of Trusses in common, with every kind of instrument for the relief and cure of Children's deformities, as Leg Irons, Spinal Stays, and Neck Swings, for crookedness of the back; Steel Backs and Collars; Dumb Bells to open the chest; Elastic Braces, &c. Advice gratis.

Morning Post and Gazetteer, **Tuesday 18 November 1800 (v.14, p.284)**

The EIGHTEENTH CENTURY took its final departure on Wednesday night. Its character, though much chequered, was, on the whole, of a glorious description. During its existence the greatest events have happened; the most important changes in the fate and fortunes of every nation in the globe have taken place. Two nations have risen to an unexampled state of prosperity, while another has undergone a revolution that has shaken nearly the whole of the universe. Poland, once great and powerful, has been dismembered, and exists no longer as an independent State. Russia and Prussia have acquired an extraordinary and unexpected importance in the scale of Continental politics. France, which in the early days of the late century, was humbled by the exertions of Britain, has in the progress of a momentous revolution, increased her power to a most gigantic and alarming extent; and England had experienced great changes and the vicissitudes of fortune. If she has lost America, in the West, she has gained an extensive and valuable dominion in the East; she has added to her naval fame, and carried the spirit of commercial enterprize to a height unexampled in the history of the world. She is now engaged in a war, in which she embarked from principle, and if the object has not been completely attained, and all her efforts have not been able to dispel the cloud which at this moment overcasts her enviable land, she has at least the high consolation, that the fidelity of her character remains unimpaired, that her honour continues unsullied, and that her national fame never, in any period of her history, shone forth with greater lustre in the eyes of the universe.

(v.15, p.128)

Preparatory steps are now taking in various parts of this town [Birmingham] for committing robberies.

Last week a black terrier dog (remarkable for his vigilance), was stolen from a house in Bull-street; and a few evenings afterwards an alarm bell was wrenched from the door of an adjoining house, and taken from the premises; at the same time a scheme was artfully laid to carry some villainous attempt into execution, by forcing a quantity of bran into the screw holes of window shutters, which would have rendered them less secure. These circumstances have been kindly mentioned to us, that the public may be upon their guard against the numerous depredators that are continually lurking about this town.

(v.15, p.187)

~

CRIMINAL INFORMATION

Mr. Gibbs moved for leave to file a Criminal Information against a person of the name of Batchelor, for writing a libellous song, reflecting on the character of certain mealmen, representing them as having arrived at Pandemonium, and seated at the Infernal Board, where the President, Lucifer, is stated to be congratulating them on the success attendant on their nefarious practices, while residing on earth, in grinding the poor, and acting their parts as griping extortioners; that now having bade adieu to the earthly paradise where they enjoyed the sweets of their ill gotten wealth, he welcomes them to regions more congenial to their native disposition, and intreats that they would consider themselves *at home*. Mr. Gibbs trusted the court would grant a Rule, this song being a libel of the most grievous tendency. Rule granted.

[NOTE: Frequent food shortages and the inflation of prices around the turn of the century led to widespread disgruntlement and occasional rioting. Poor crops were partly to blame, but often anger was vented at mealmen, who (it was believed) stockpiled wheat and flour to drive up prices.]

c. **November 1801 (v.15, p.289)**

~

DOCTOR'S COMMONS, JULY 7

CRIM. CON.

This was a suit instituted by Ann Kirby against Francis Kirby, Esq. her husband, for a restitution of conjugal rites. The defendant pleaded, that his wife had been guilty of adultery; and the wife retorted the accusation. The case was altogether of a very uncommon complexion.

It appeared the parties had resided formerly at a place called Winterbrook, from whence Mrs. Kirby had eloped, in consequence, as she inferred in her allegations, of the defendants conduct towards her. After a considerable absence, she commenced these proceedings, to compel her husband to cohabit with her. To repel her suit, he charged her with acts of adultery with a person of the name of Bouchee; and also, with a Mr. Fruin; and lastly, with a Captain Master. With respect to the latter, it was alleged, that the Captain used to come down to his house in his absence, and pretending before the servants that he was suddenly taken ill, would request leave to retire to lay down; that the lady, pitying his state, would desire the bed to be got ready for him, and then attend on him with some warm restorative; that she was generally a very considerable period using her benevolent endeavours to sooth and console him, and that upon such occasions the bed afterwards exhibited marks of disorder not altogether justifying the idea of a single person in a weak state of body having lain in it; that, after her Samaritan disposition had been exercised for two or three hours, and she had poured the oil of affection into the Captain's wounded soul, he generally rose fresh as the vernal morn. The Captain was so often sick, so often put to bed, and so often attended to by his fair Hygeia, that the superstitions of the husband were aroused …

Bell's Weekly Messenger, **Saturday 12 July 1801 (v.15, p.303)**

Garnerin lately sent up a balloon near Petersburg, with a parachute attached to it, containing a cat.

At a certain height a lighted match set fire to the balloon, and the cat descended to earth in the parachute unhurt.

[NOTE: Luckily for the cat, André-Jacques Garnerin was the inventor of the frameless parachute, and had successfully completed his first descent six years earlier.]

c. July 1803 (v.16, p.175)

Hints to the seconds in duels:

With a little water you must make some gunpowder into a fine paste, then roll it into balls, dry them, and rub them over with pencil, to give them the appearance of lead; these you must substitute for those brought for your principles: - Remember, in ramming them down you must break them into dust. You should also take the opportunity of giving the hat of one of the combatants a hard pinch with a bullet mould. After the parties have fired, which will have been as is the custom, together, you must shew the mark and swear you saw the bullet strike, and with great warmth insist upon it, that not only must the wearer have heard the ball, but also have felt his hat shake. You must not allow him to deny it, if he should do so at first, which is very improbable, he will not do so long. The writer having practiced it more than once with a happy success, he now recommends it to those gentlemen who may be engaged to see their friends fight, and do not wish them to commit murder.

The Derby Mercury, **Thursday 27 October 1803 (v.16, p.230)**

~

SKETCH OF A RUSSIAN

NOBLEMAN

BY E.D. CLARKE, LLD

Some of the Nobles are much richer than the riches of our English peers, and a vast number, as may be supposed, are very poor. To this poverty, and these riches, are equally joined the most abject meanness, and the most detestable profligacy. In sensuality, they are without limits of the law, conscience, or honour. The toys of infants, the baubles of French fops, constitutes the highest object of their wishes. Novelty delights the human race, but no part of it seeks for it so eagerly as the Russian Nobles. Novelty in their debaucheries, novelty in their gluttony, novelty in cruelty, novelty in whatever they pursue. This is not the case with the lower class, who preserve their habits unaltered from one generationto another. But there are characteristics in which the Russian Prince and the Russian Peasant are the same. They are all equally barbarous. Visit a Russian, of whatever rank, at his country seat, and you will find him lounging about, uncombed, unwashed, unshaved, half naked, eating raw turnips, and drinking *quofs*. The raw turnip is handed about in slices in the first houses on a silver salver with brandy, as a whet before dinner. Their hair is universally in a state not to be described, and their bodies only to be divested of vermin when they frequent the bath.

[NOTE: Describing the luxuries of the Russian table, Dr Clarke says – 'If the visitor ventures, which he should avoid if he is hungry, to inspect the soup in his plate with too inquisitive an eye, he will doubtless discern living victims in distress, which a Russian if he saw would swallow with indifference.']

c. 1810, printed extract from *Travels in Various Countries … *Dr E.D. Clarke (v.17, p.1)

Tuesday the Otter hounds of Mr. Coleman of Leominster, killed in Monkland mill-pond, an otter of extraordinary size; it measured from the nose to the end of the tail four feet ten inches, and weighed $34\frac{1}{2}$lb. This animal was supposed to be nearly 8 years old, and to have destroyed a ton of fish yearly.

The Derby Mercury, **Thursday 17 May 1804 (v.17, p.41)**

GREENWICH PARK – The fineness of the day drew vast crowds of holiday folks to Greenwich, where, as usual, rolling down the hill was the chief amusement of the evening, when they adjourned to the public houses in the neighbourhood, and, to use their own phrase, 'kept it up till a late hour;' some joining in the festive dance, others paying court to *Bacchus*. Not a few were incapable of finding their way home again; and many a simple girl, who left their master's house with a good reputation, has commenced a career of infamy and misery.

The Morning Post, Tuesday 3 April 1804 (v.17, p.47)

Lord Chesterfield said, 'A good set of teeth, in either sex, must considerably add to the prepossessions formed in the mind on a first appearance.' – And the observation acquires additional force from the circumstance of the generality of the English nation, from their mode of living, being troubled with scurvy in the gums, which produces tooth-ache, and eventually rotten teeth. These disagreeable effects may be prevented by the timely use of *Bulter's Restorative Tooth Powder*, which is used by the Queen and Princesses. It imparts a firmness and beautiful redness to the gums, to the breath the most delectable sweetness, to the teeth a pearly whiteness, restores the enamel, fills up the cavities, and prevents the dreadful effects of tooth-ache.

Various (v.17, p.56)

❖

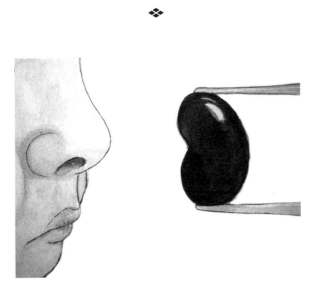

The following singular circumstance is stated as fact. The child of a Mr. Wright, of Duke-street, Manchester-square, for some time past complained of a pain in its nostrils, which appeared quite flat, and the parents were of the opinion that she had broken her nose by a fall; her forehead was become black. A surgeon examined and probed the nostril, and drew from thence a *kidney bean*, swelled four times as big as its common size when dry, and which had begun to grow in the child's head, striking upwards. It was extracted perfect, except splitting in half. Mr. Wright has it preserved in spirits. The child, which is three years of age, must, it is supposed, have pushed it up in playing with it.

c. **July 1804 (v.17, p.63)**

Woodcote Lodge, the seat of Mr. Durand, was yesterday the scene of sport and festivity. At one o'clock a badger, of uncommon powers, was put into a hole, and after several unsuccessful attempts by other dogs, was at length most gallantly drawn by Mr. Durand's dog *Bully*.

[NOTE: Though badger baiting was legal until 1835, it was not without its critics. Thomas Young in his *Essay on Humanity to Animals* condemned it, along with bear-baiting, cock-fighting, hunting, shooting and fishing. He examines the historical precedents, and notes: 'If any nation were to be brought as an instance of the tendency of cruel sports and bloody spectacles to instil courage into the spectators, I suppose the Romans would be pitched upon. But then we must recollect that such spectacles never became common among them till after the defeat of Hannibal; and no one will say that the Romans improved either in valour or virtue after that era.' *An essay on Humanity to Animals* by Thomas Young, London, 1798, pp. 71–2.]

Jackson's Oxford Journal, Saturday 2 June 1804 (v.17, p.65)

~

BY ROYAL AUTHORITY

Dr. Gardner's
WORM MUSEUM
NOW OPEN FOR THE INSPECTION OF
MEDICAL MEN AND THE PUBLIC AT LARGE,
At Long-Acre, near Bow-street;
No. 3, High-street, Shoreditch; and at his son's
house; High-street, Birmingham.

Price 4s. 6d. – 10s. 6d. – or 21s. a box.

There never has yet appeared in this Country, nor perhaps in any other, such an unparalleled Collection of the Wonders of Nature as these Museums contain; all of which were expelled from the bodies of persons who are principally now in health, and are happy to testify the same; in which are Worms from 1 inch to 500 feet in length, some with 150 mouths, others in form of Caterpillars and Beetles; another species like Wood-lice, 12 feet to each; a Wolf from the stomach, expelled from a Lady at Hoxton, who had nearly fallen a victim to its ravages for three years; one animal with ears like a Mouse, and mouth like a Flounder, from a man; another with 4 horns, 6 legs and 12 feet, which lived nine days; the Lizard of the Stomach, from Mrs. H., Bedford-street, Covent-garden, a long small body, with a head resembling a Cat; 80 Worms, resembling Shrimps from a male, who had been in a bad state of health, but speedily recovered after they had been expelled; a curious worm of the Tænia species, 30 feet in length. – Miss ---, Tottenham-court-road, fell into a deep decline, attended with a voracious appetite; if the cravings of nature were not satisfied she soon fainted, and a general lassitude and debility took place; she obtained relief by voiding, according to her own assertion, 20,000 small worms; the young lady now enjoys a good state of health.

These form but a small and incomplete specimen of the contents of the Museums; an infinity of other animals equally astonishing are exhibited. – What idea can be formed of the ravages which the Vermicular tribes, in their varied species, commit on the human frame?

(v.17, p.82)

A weaver of the name McAdam, residing at Killearn, Stirlingshire, fired on the 10th Sept. at a covey of partridges, but the shot expelled backwards the dock of the piece with a long prong through his forehead into the brain, in the line of the *frontal rupture*, where it remained. He tugged it side to side, till he got it extracted, and then he ran nearly a quarter of a mile, and sent for a surgeonto dress it, who perceived some brain upon the dock, and the pulsation of the brain through the aperture. The unfortunate man continued sensible till within two days of his death. The brain began to obtrude on the 2nd of Oct. and on the 14th, a portion of it, about an inch in diameter, and two inches long, came away with the dressing. He became totally insensible on Thursday the 18th, his pulse then at 120, and was seized with a universal quivering, which continued till his death on the 20th.

c. **November 1810 (v.19, p.9)**

~

SUSSEX ASSIZES

HORSHAM, MONDAY, MARCH 21.
INDECENT BATHING
The King v. John Crundon
The defendant was indicted for indecently exposing himself on the 26th of June, and 2nd of July last.

Mr. Gurney having opened the indictment, Mr. Serjeant Shepherd stated the circumstances of the case. He observed, that it had long been the practise of various persons to undress and bathe so near to the houses and within view of the inhabitants of the town of Brighton, that at length many respectable persons had associated themselves into a committee to prevent such an indecent nuisance. They had accordingly met and pointed out the limits within which persons not using machines might bathe in the sea, and in general most persons acquiesced in their resolution. Notwithstanding these different accommodations the defendant, who was a tailor at Brighton, refused to conform to these reasonable regulations, but obstinately persisted in the indecent practice of bathing within a few yards of the houses. He had been frequently remonstrated with, but his uniform answer was, *the sea was free*, and he would bathe when and where he pleased. Nor was he merely content in doing this in his own person, but he had induced many other people to follow his example, and he constantly came at the head of his companions, by whom he was denominated the Captain, and in defiance of all decency and remonstrance, daily exposed himself naked on the beach. The Learned Serjeant observed, it imported to the character of the town to prevent such practices, inasmuch as no decent man could suffer the female part of his family to walk abroad if their eyes were to be offended with such gross practices.

The Morning Chronicle, **Thursday 23 March 1809**
(v.19, p.37)

~

BATHING TRUSSES

It has been advised by the most eminent Surgeon, that persons affected with a Hernia should not bathe without a Truss. They have hitherto been prevented in consequence of spoiling their Trusses. SALMON, ODY and Co, beg leave to inform their friends and the Public that their much approved PATENT SELF-ADJUSTING TRUSSES are now manufactured water-proof. In consequence of the superiority of their invention, the patentees have received the following appointments:-

His Majesty's Royal Navy, the Royal Naval Hospitals and Dockyards, the Ordnance, Greenwich Hospital, the Hon. East India Company &etc.

Manufactory, 292, Strand.

Persons residing in the Country, sending their circumference of the body, in inches, just above the hips, may depend on being accurately fitted.

Various, *c.* 1813–16 (v.26, p.40)

~

EXTRAORDINARY

NAVAGATOR

A fine tortoiseshell cat was on Friday morning seen approaching London Bridge, peaceably seated in a large bowl dish. As she advanced towards the fall, every one anticipated she would be overturned and precipitated into the stream. She kept her seat, however, with great presence of mind, and amidst loud cheers, shot the centre arch with as much dexterity as the most experienced waterman. A boy hearing her voice shortly after she had made this hazardous attempt, and fancying she wanted a *pilot*, rowed towards her and took her into his wherry, when he found around her neck a parchment scroll, stating that if she should reach London in safety, that she should be conveyed to a Mrs. Clarke in Highstreet, Borough, who would reward the bringer. The boy conveyed poor puss to Mrs. Clarke, who seemed to be apprised of the circumstance, and rewarded the messenger with half a crown. It

turned out that the voyage was undertaken for a wager between two Richmond gentlemen, and that puss embarked at the turn of the tide in the course of the night, and happily reached her destination without sustaining any injury.

Caledonian Mercury, **Thursday 2 September 1813 (v.26, p.43a)**

On Tuesday se'night was taken on the shore of the Solway, near Bowness, by Christopher Robinson, a fisherman, one of those curious productions of Nature of the order Zoophytes, known by the general name of Sea Polypi. The substance of this creature is very gelatinous, and consists chiefly of eight long arms, studded with war-like tubercles, with which it adheres to rocks &etc. The head, in which are inserted two large eyes, is in the centre of the body, and the mouth is diametrically underneath; in the centre of the arms is the passage by which the aliment is discharged. The anterior extremity of the polypus consists of a very large bag, for the purpose of containing a black liquid, which, when assailed, it discharges and, discolouring the water, eludes observation.

The Morning Chronicle, Thursday 16 September 1813 (v.26, p.78)

James Hall stood indicted for having stolen a sheep, the property of Benjamin Hopkinson and James Manfield.

Mr. Hopkinson joined Mr. Mansfield in the purchase of some sheep, which were kept near

Highgate; one was a little black sheep. Witness recognised the head and two quarters of this sheep in the field, on the day after it was stolen.

A watchman proved his having taken the prisoner into custody, and having found on his person two quarters, which were compared, in the presence of the prosecutor, with the remaining parts of the sheep, and found to correspond.

c. January 1814 (v.28, p.41)

A few weeks since Mrs. Polito, relict of the late keeper of the Menagerie, at Exeter 'Change, departed this life at an advanced age. Since her death a lion, a tiger, and a wolf, have died in succession.

[NOTE: Sarah Polito was the wife, and subsequent widow, of lauded menagerist Stephan Polito. Their animal collection was visited by Byron, who was so impressed by Chunee the elephant that he 'wished he was my butler'. *Letters and Journals*, 3.206.]

c. August 1814 (v.30, p.170)

Another most extraordinary affair has happened in the high life, which is likely to engage the public attention. A *Peeress* was detected on Monday last in a situation most unequivocal, by her injured Lord, who, in the height of passion, discharged a pistol at the inamorata, and shot him through the arm, which is said to be fractured. It happened near Staines.

The Hull Packet and Original Weekly Commercial,
Literary and General Advisor, Tuesday 14 February
(St Valentine's Day), 1815 (v.30, p.227)

Mr. Sadler, of Bentham, about four miles from Cheltenham, had last week a sow which he intended to farry (or pig) before morning – it consequently became necessary that someone should sit up; the two maid servants agreed to do so, and in the middle of the night the dogs began barking; the girls with great presence of mind took up their master's gun and fired it; the master called out at the window to know what was the matter; they told him that some man had been in the yard and ran away; about an hour afterwards, the girls saw two men, (the gun having been re-charged) they fired at them, and the men ran away. Mr. S., in the morning, went to the place where the men were seen, and found the fowls pent up, with the intention (it is assumed) of stealing them. A duck was found with its head cut off.

c. **February 1815 (v.30, p.260)**

A few days ago, a little girl, about twelve years of age, walked deliberately into the sea, near Sunderland pier, and attempted to drown herself. A pilot observing her, rushed into the watery elements and brought her safe on shore. On questioning the child as to the cause for her attempt at suicide, she declared that it was in consequence of her mother insisting upon her *learning to write*, and obliging her to provide money to pay for her instruction, by gathering sticks.

The Morning Chronicle, **Tuesday 31 January 1815 (v.30, p.263)**

~

DRURY LANE

We are absolutely wearied with the dullness and absurdity of our Theatres. Piece after piece is produced, and still nothing consolatory or reviving. Nothing appears upon which we can risqué a serious comment – nothing to call forth any other feelings than anger or contempt: last night this Theatre added to the unprofitable list, another piece of heavy improbability, under the title of *The Unknown Guest*. Would it had ever remained unknown, at least to us! Of story this piece has none, but there are certain jumps and jerks of what is intended to be a sort of narrative. Mr. Braham is a mysterious, remorseful kind of villainous hero, in a pair of sky-blue pantaloons, and short shirt sleeves. His name is *Rodolf*, and by the very novel contrivance of making him save a young girl he is introduced into a castle, the son of whose owner and brother of his mistress he is supposed to have murdered. Here he sings a good many songs, and does a sufficient number of unaccountable things – he conceals much that were better known, and places himself in unnecessary difficulties, these are, of course, all removed, and though every soul in the drama labours to counteract common nature, and probability, yet in the end, all turns out as it should do.

We might, perhaps, as well merely have said, that there are a great many scenes, all merely preparatory to the last – the explosion of a mine, and the destruction of a tower, which appears to be considered not only the strength of the piece, but as capable of superseding every other requisite. The dialogue is wretched, and the poetry worse, and the music, for the greater part appeared to be worthy of both. Where it pretended to be original, it frequently exhibited the most palpable plagiarisms; and even where the stolen idea had originally been beautiful, either alteration or misapplication had destroyed all its pristine spirit. The fresh tender fragrant leaves of spring, when become the food of caterpillars, are changed to excrement.

Perhaps no piece of the original music will survive the next three months; and in this particular there is a happy coincidence between that and the words – they will find their euthanasia in each other's arms.

c. **April 1815** (v.30, p.299)

~

ARTIFICIAL TEETH

A PROFESSIONAL GENTLEMAN having been long in the habit of using Artificial teeth, had his mind naturally turned to the various qualities and different kinds in use, in order to determine the preference. He found that those made of the sea-horse [walrus] are very corruptible, and apt to taint the Breath; human Teeth set in a frame are little better, and liable to loosen in a short time. The Mineral Paste Teeth are free from these defects, but their opacity and dreadness render them no deception; they are discernable in every wearer, and besides, have a strong tendency to lose their polish and turn black. He conceived, therefore, that if he could form a substance pellucid, susceptible of various tinges, and of sufficient hardness to retain its colour and polish, it would be superior to them all. A knowledge of chemistry has enabled him to bring it to perfection, so that his teeth are a perfect Representation of Natural Teeth, with the advantage of imbibing no water, and suffering no change from time.

Mr George Spence; Dentist to his majesty.

The Morning Chronicle, Sunday 28 May 1815
(v.31, p.144)

IN ENGLAND MORE PEOPLE GET BALD or
their hair turn grey at an earlier age than in any
other country, therefore Prince's Genuine Russia
Oil ought to be generally used, for it is the best and
wholesomest Oil for the hair of Ladies, Gentlemen,
and Children, and if used constantly not a hair will
fall off or turn grey; where hair has got thin or bald,
in the least roots, will be restored. Gentlemen who
use powder ought to wear it as pomatum.

Various, *c.* 1816–19 (v.31, p.169)

An antique fragment of Greek Architecture, of
enlarged dimensions, and in an exquisite style, is to
be seen at a stone-cutter's in the new road. It was
brought to London by Lord Elgin, and is supposed

to have been the identical pedestal on which was placed the Triton on the apex of the marble roof of the tower of Andronicus Cyrrhestes at Athens, commonly called the Tower of the Winds. It has the appearance of a capital to a column, and is about three feet in diameter, and in one piece of the purest white marble. It is said to be consigned to the mason, to make chimney pieces for Lord Elgin's new house.

The Morning Chronicle, **Saturday 28 September 1811 (v.32, p.9)**

~

SURPRISING MONKIES

FROM PARIS

Continuing to be received by crowded audiences with most enthusiastic applause and approbation, will, with the following Entertainments, be repeated every evening this week. The Public are most respectfully informed, that in order to avoid disappointment, the Monkies commence their performance at half past six to a minute.

The Morning Chronicle **and various, January 1817**
(v.34, p.1)

~

DISGRACEFUL TRANSACTION

A man, a few days since, sold his wife, in a halter, for 1s. 6d. in the public market, at Wellington, and allowed the purchaser a quart of ale to drink his health.

Jackson's Oxford Journal, **Saturday 8 February 1817**
(v.34, p.8)

~

FOX CHACE

On Saturday last the hounds of J. MABERLY, Esq. started a fox in Old Park, Godstone, Surrey, that afforded the huntsmen uncommonly fine sport. He ran from thence to Laghan's Wood, a distance of ten miles, when he dashed through the covers to Stockhurst, and took the road to Lampfield, but being closely pursued, he took shelter on the roof of a low cottage, where a butcher's dog attempted to dislodge him. The distressed situation of poor *Reynard* claimed the attention of the head huntsman of the pack, a true sportsman, and he instantly called off the hounds, to allow a short time for the fox to recover himself, but *Reynard*, rather ungrateful for this indulgence, seemed not disposed again to renew the chace, and the sport was now quite at a stand-still. The whipper in was compelled to flog him three times round the cottage chimney before he could make the *sly one* start.

Jackson's Oxford Journal, **Saturday 8 February 1817**
(v.34, p.8)

ROBBERY ON THE RIVER

On Sunday night, between ten and twelve o'clock, two chests of indigo, and a quantity of paper, was stolen from a barge lying off Trigg's Wharf, Thames-street. One chest of the indigo was found next morning on shore, off King's Arms Stairs, Westminster. It is supposed one of the robbers cut himself in getting at the paper, as what remained behind was stained with blood.

(**v.34, p.22**)

The Sapient Pig, the greatest curiosity of the present day will be at home on Monday next, when he will exhibit, for a few weeks, his wonderful abilities in the knowledge of letters, figures, and cards, with which he will ſpell and read, cast accounts, play at cards, tell the hour of the day, the age of any person present and their thoughts, with

many other novelties, at the Royal Rooms, Spring-gardens, Charring-cross. The hours of performance commence precisely at eleven, twelve and one o'clock; again at four; and again in the evening at six and seven. Admittance: 1s.

Hail, Toby! truly sapient Pig!
Most worthy of a wig,
Or any other decoration
Befitting best a learned vocation.
Thy look intelligent surpasses
The vacant stare of human Asses;

Thy grunts more real knowledge speak,
Than thousands have who smatter Greek.

The Morning Chronicle, 14 July 1817 (v.40, p.91)

≈

SADLER'S WELLS

Yesterday evening this theatre commenced its operations for the season, and immediately after its doors were opened, was crowded to excess in every quarter. The rush into the pit and galleries was so violent, that several accidents occurred in both places before the spectators were enabled to secure their seats. Those which happened in the pit are such as will only occasionto whom they befell, a temporary inconvenience; but those which happened in the gallery are of a more serious nature, and are more likely to be attended with lasting consequences. The crowd which frequented this part of the house, were all so eager to obtain seats first, that no obstacle seemed capable to retard, and no danger sufficient to deter them in their efforts to secure them. A young lad, between 16 and 17 years of age, in hurrying down the space between the benches, chanced to fall, and was in consequence trampled to death. Some of the individuals who had obtained seats in the front row, were pushed over the iron balustrade into the pit, but fortunately escaped without any other harm than that of receiving some severe contusions. The performance commenced, notwithstanding the fatal accident which had happened, at the time at which they had been announced on the playbill. In the interval between the acts several Amazons in the gallery, who appeared to have been indulging in large portions of something stronger than beer, afforded a high treat to the gentlemen of fancy who were in the theatre, by an exhibition of their pugilistic powers. If these little skirmishes be not taken into account, the audience were, after the first uproar had subsided, tolerably quiet for an Easter Monday evening.

c. 1818–20 (v.41, p.12)

~

MANCHESTER

STEAM CARRIAGE – (From a correspondent) – An ingenious cotton-spinner of Ardwick, near this town, has invented a *locomotive* steam carriage, for the conveyance of goods or passengers without the aid of horses. After repeated experiments during the last two years, he has so far succeeded, as not to leave a doubt that it will answer the purposes intended. It will go upon any of the mail roads *up hill* or *down*, at the rate of nine or ten miles an hour, and can be guided with the greatest ease, on the most difficult roads. (We have heard that a worthy couple, on their way from Stockport to this town, were nearly frightened out of their wits by meeting this machine during a trial of its powers, which, for obvious reasons, was made in the dark: indeed, it was enough to appal the stoutest heart, to see a carriage of extraordinary shape, and carrying a glowing fire, and moving at a tremendous rate, without any apparent means of propulsion.)

The Morning Chronicle, 7 November 1821 (v.50, p.19)

~

ROYAL REGULATIONS

The following regulations are given in a manuscript regulating the household of Henry VIII: - His Highness's baker shall not put alums in the bread, or mix rye, oaten, or bean flour with the same; and if detected, he shall be put in the stocks. His Highness's attendants are not to steal the locks or keys, or tables, cupboards, or any other furniture, out of nobleman's, or any other gentleman's houses when he goes to visit. Master-cooks shall not employ such Scullions as go about naked, or lie all night before the kitchen fire. Dinners to be at ten, suppers at four. The officers of his Privy Chamber shall be loving together: no grudging or grumbling, nor talking of the King's pastime. The king's barber is enjoined to be cleanly, – not to frequent the company of misguided women, for fear of danger to the King's royal person. There shall be no romping with maids on the staircase, by which dishes and other things are often broken.

[NOTE: Though this dubious manuscript has not been traced to a modern collection, it appears to have been exceedingly popular at the time. Quotes from it appear also in *The Literary Panorama* (1816) and *The Mirror of Literature, Amusement and Instruction* (1828), in both cases with the addendum that the king's brewers are 'not to put any brimstone in the ale'.]

c. November 1821 (v.50, p.26)

~

SINGULAR NAVAL

COSTUME

The officers of the Swedish Navy are considered military officers, and in full dress are obliged to wear spurs! It used to excite the surprise of our officers, on walking aft, to see the captain of the ship strutting about the quarter-deck with spurs on. As to the jack tars, it put them in such a rage they would have advised a war with Sweden to oblige the king to lay by the offensive costume, which irritated and offended them in a great degree.

'The Mirror of Fashion' in *The Morning Chronicle*, Tuesday 20 November 1821 (v.50, p.84)

≈

WAYS AND MEANS

GLASGOW – A young girl in this neighbourhood, in the prospect of marriage, being unable to find money to purchase wedding-clothes, a few days ago actually submitted to having five front teeth drawn, for which she received five guineas, and purchased the necessary articles.

The Times, Tuesday 20 November 1821 (v.50, p.85)

~

POLICE

Mansion House. A man named *Thompson* was yesterday brought before the LORD MAYOR, on a charge of having stolen a pair of mud-pipes, or heavy boots.

The complainant stated, that he was at work in America-square cleaning the sewers, and had left his mud-pipes close by. On turning round he saw the prisoner take them up, hand one to an accomplice, and run off. He immediately pursued them, and took the prisoner into custody. The other escaped with the odd boot.

The prisoner said he had been a long time in great distress, and had tried every where to get work, but without success. He had even offered his labour for food alone, and was refused: he then had no thing left but to starve or to steal, and he thought any thing better than dying.

The prisoner was asked why, if his distress was so great as he had described, he had not preferred robbing a baker's shop, instead of stealing leather, which he could not easily feed upon.

Prisoner – My Lord, I can prove that I have robbed a number of baker's shops, and that I was watching one a long time before I took the boots, but could get no opportunity. I have lived in that way more than a week.

The complainant said he was so poor that he could not afford to prosecute, and the LORD MAYOR committed the prisoner as a common pilferer, found at large without any means of obtaining his livelihood, and sentenced him to be imprisoned two months in Bridewell, to be kept to hard labour, and well whipped.

The Times, Friday 28 November 1821 (v.50, p.104)

~

GALVANIC PHENOMENA

The body of George Thom, who was executed at Aberdeen last week, having, agreeably to his sentence, been given for dissection to Drs. Skene and Ewing, was subjected to a series of galvanic experiments, of which, with their results, we subjoin the following brief account: - The Body was brought into the dissecting room about an hour after suspension, and still retained nearly its natural heat. The upper part of the spinal cord and the sciatic nerve were immediately laid bare, and a galvanic area was then established by applying the positive wire to the spine, and the negative to the sciatic nerve, whereby a general convulsive starting of the body was produced. Another communication was then made between the spine and the ulnar nerve, and considerable contractions took place in the arm and fore-arm. When the circle was formed with the spine and the radial nerve, both at the elbow and wrist successively, powerful contractions of the muscles of the whole arm were produced. The hand was closed with such violence, as to resist the exertions of one assistant to keep it open. When a connexion was established between the radial nerve and the supra and infra orbital nerves, strong contractions of the muscles of the brow, face and mouth, were produced, so as to affect the under jaw, and to distort the countenance in a very singular manner. The eye-lids were strongly contracted; and when the wire was applied directly to the ball of the eye, the iris contracted very sensibly. The tongue was also moved in all directions, by touching the surface with the galvanic wire. The whole experiment was performed in about an hour and a quarter, when the heat of the body was considerably diminished. A powerful galvanic apperatus (consisting of about 300 pairs of plates) was used; but from not being insulated a great quantity of the galvanism escaped; so that every metallic substance around the table was highly charged.

Caledonian Mercury, **Monday 26 November 1821**
(v.50, p.118)

~

QUEEN MAB

From a correspondent:
The Vice-Suppression Society has instituted two prosecutions for the publication of the entire poem

(with all its notes) of *Queen Mab*, by Percy Bysshe Shelley. The indictments are against the publisher, W. Clark, 201 Strand. The following are two of the thirteen passages selected for prosecution.

Spirit of Nature! All-suffering power,
Necessity! Thou mother of the world!
Unlike the God of human error, thou
Requirest no prayers or praises; the caprice
Of man's weak will belongs no more to thee
Than do the changeful passions of his breast.
[p.58]

Note vii, p.149: 'Analogy seems to favour the opinion, that as, like other systems, Christianity has arisen and augmented, so, like them, it will decay and perish, &c.'

The author was not 18 when he wrote 'Queen Mab'.

The Times, Tuesday 11 December 1821 (v.50, p.184)

~

DISTRESSING OCCURRENCE

On Saturday last some families living on Navy Island, in the Niagara river, had made preparations for removing to the Canada shore, and had loaded a boat with their household effects. The wind rising to a considerable height, it was thought imprudent, by some of the party, to attempt crossing so near the falls with the wind blowing down the stream. Some of them consequently refused to embark; but three men, more bold, or less considerate than the rest went aboard for the purpose of crossing, but thinking it proper to wait a little for the falling of the wind they all laid down to sleep. During this time the rising of the water, or some other cause, loosened the boat from its moorings, and these unfortunate men soon found themselves fast approaching the rapids which lead to the main falls. No human power could now save them and they were precipitated into the eternal world by one of the most awful deaths it is possible to conceive. Many of their goods were seen floating below the falls much broken to pieces, except a dining table which floated ashore uninjured.

c. November 1821 (v.50, p.188)

A Mr. Smith was attacked at night, about a fortnight ago, in the neighbourhood of Hexam, by three men, who dragged him from his horse, and threw him on the ground face downwards. They made no attempt to rob him, nor did they utter a syllable. Mr Smith also held his tongue until feeling the teeth of a saw enter into the flesh at the back of his neck, he exclaimed – 'What are you doing with me?' On hearing his voice, one of the men observed with an oath – 'It is not him!' And all three immediately departed. These barbarians had obviously been upon the look-out for some object of revenge, whom they had intended to destroy by means of the instrument we have mentioned.

The Times, **Wednesday 19 December 1821**
(v.50, p.223)

As an interesting appendage to observations, we inset a passage from 'Robinson's memoirs of the Mexican Revolution,' descriptive of the means of opening a direct passage by canal between the Atlantic and Pacific, through the Mexican isthmus. The preference, we find, is here given to the lake of Nicaragua over the Gulf of Panama; and it is impossible to contemplate, without a mixture of awe and exultation the practical, nay, it would seem, the approaching accomplishment of a work which would unite the billows of two mighty oceans, and by an easy process of human labour and enterprise, change, as it were the physical boundaries of the world:

'We now come to treat a section of the American continent where the magnificent scheme of cutting a navigable canal, between the two oceans, appears unencumbered with any natural obstacles.

'The province of Costa Rica, or, as it is named by some geographers, Nicaragua, has occupied but the very cursory notice of either Spanish or other writers; they have all, however, stated, that a communication could be opened by the lake of Nicaragua, between *the two seas, but no accurate description of the country has ever been published; and indeed so completely has the mind of the public been turned towards the isthmus of Panama as the favoured spot where the canal should be cut, that Costa Rica has been disregarded.'*

c. 1821–3 (v.50, p.268)

The mode of courtship in some parts of Fife is curious. When a young man hath the felicity to be invited of the same party with the maiden who hath won his affections, then doth he endeavour to sit opposite her at the table, where he giveth himself up not to those unseemly oglings and gazing which be practiced in other parts, to the offence of aged virgins and other persons of much discretion; but putting forth his foot, he presseth and treadeth on the feet and toes of the maiden; whereupon if she do not roar forth, it is a sign that his addresses are well received, and the two come in due course before the minister. This form of attack is known by the name of

Footie, and the degree of pressure doth denote the warmth of the passion. Such men as be bashful do take with them a more forward friend who shall, vicariously, and in their stead, give a light pressure and treading.

The Times, Wednesday 2 January 1822 (v.51, p.15)

GUILDHALL – Two young men of respectable appearance, were brought yesterday before the sitting Magistrate, Mr Alderman Birch, on separate charges, for disturbing peaceable families in their beds by violently ringing the doorbells in the dead of night. The first of these gentlemen was caught by the watchman of Castle-baynardward, in the act of ringing Mr. Harris's bell, and the latter by the watchman of St. Bride's parish, performing a similar trick at Messrs. Taylor and Hessey's, in Fleet-street.

The prisoners pleaded, as their only excuse, inebriety; and protested that this was the first and only time they had been guilty of the offence alleged against them.

Mr. Alderman Birch reprobated in strong terms the mischief and folly of this practise, in which young men, in a state of intoxication, were frequently indulging themselves.

c. **Wednesday 2 January 1822 (v.51, p.14)**

A FORTUNE HUNTER

One of those minions of Cupid, being in a ball-room at Bath, heard a gentleman giving an account of the death of a rich old widow thus: - 'Died yesterday, in her 89th year' said the narrator. 'What a pity!' exclaimed the fortune hunter, 'what a fine match she would have made two days ago!'

Liverpool Mercury, **Friday 8 January 1822 (v.51, p.52)**

We have heard that all the instruments of coercion formally used in Ilchester gaol, such as thumb-screws, body-irons, male and female stocks, &c., have been laid aside by Mr. Hardy, the present keeper, who considers them as unnecessary.

The Examiner, **Sunday 20 January 1822 (v.51, p.81)**

~

SHIP NEWS

The confectioners have been able to lay in a store of ice to freeze their creams this summer! If the frost had not favoured them last week they might have been obliged to send, as heretofore, to the coast of Greenland for a cargo; but their last venture of that kind, six years ago, was, like every speculation in a slippery commodity, attended with such risk, that it has made them averse from repeating the experiment. When the cargo arrived in the river, the Custom-house officers were, as usual, on the alert, and the ice-berg from which it had been abstracted clearly not having either a custom-house or an accompting-house erected upon it, the customary bills of landing and clearance were wanting. This was not the only informality discovered in the case. The commodity being foreign, it was clear it should be entered at the custom house of London; but whether under the head of *produce*, or *manufacture*, was a very puzzling question. After much dispute, it was proposed to cut the knot, by entering the commodity as *foreign fabric*; and not being enumerated in the custom house list, it was consigned to pay a duty *ad valorem*. The duty *ad valorem*, our commercial readers know, is 25 per cent., and the importer has the option of estimating the value. A compromise was, however, effected, in time to prevent a premature dissolution: and the remnants of the precarious commodity were distributed amongst the ice-houses in town.

The Examiner, **Sunday 20 January 1822 (v.51, p.95)**

Some time ago, a young woman of interesting appearance, named Ann Dartnell, was tried at the

Old Bailey for stealing, and convicted upon pretty clear evidence. Her misfortune attracted the notice of Mr. Williams, of Smithfield, the last Sheriff, who calculated very strongly upon the influence of an act of kindness upon the poor convict, and expressed his readiness to become her friend, and place her in a state above the reach of want. She was so overcome by the generosity of the proposal as to be unable to give vent to her gratitude in the usual way, but she thanked her benefactor with her tears, which Mr. Williams looked upon as a more sure test of sincerity than the language of the tongue. He forthwith directed that she should be received as a servant into his own family. The order was obeyed, and Ann Dartnell was soon as confidently employed as if she had been introduced to Mr. Williams on the most unquestionable recommendations. Her conduct was observed to be distinguished by strong marks of attachment to her master and family; but one morning she took it into her head to rise earlier than usual, and to walk out with a bundle containing not only her own clothes, but a great quantity of plate. Her master, upon missing his silver, tea, table and dessert spoons, forks, sugar dishes, snuffers, gold thimble, and other articles of considerable value, and finding that his new servant was missing at the same time, concluded that Ann Dartnell had not improved in the degree he expected. He forthwith ordered that the police should be informed of the facts, and that handbills should be printed, describing the persona and face of the ungrateful servant, and offering 15 guineas to any person who should cause her apprehension and conviction. The handbills state that she is 24 years of age and in the family way.

c. 5–6 March 1822 (v.51, p.271)

Coffee and **Chocolate** made in **one minute** by D. Dunn's essence of coffee and cocoa nut, sold by F. Graham, corner of Belle Sauvage-Inn, Ludgate Hill in half pint bottles, and the chocolate in pots. Directions for use: - Put a teaspoonful of either of these essences in a cup, with the usual proportion of milk and sugar, and fill it with boiling water and you have instantaneously a cup of coffee or chocolate of exquisite flavour. From the ease and expedition attending this invention, it becomes a valuable acquisitionto the public, and more especially to officers of the army and navy, to captains of vessels, travellers, innkeepers, public assemblies, and particularly to ladies or gentlemen not keeping an establishment. Trade supplied.

The Morning Chronicle, c. **March 1822 (v.52, p.5)**

INDIGESTION – PLUMBE and HALL'S DIGESTIVE, or DINNER PILLS furnish an effectual antidote to this universal evil, and give the proprietors daily proof of their efficacy in a variety of complaints with which it is accompanied, as bilious afflictions, flatulence, nausea, oppression of the chest, pain in the stomach, habitual costiveness, giddiness, and head-ache &c. By the use of these many are restored to health and comfort who, through a weak and impaired state of health, were debarred even the ordinary enjoyment of life. They contain no calomel, are of a character quite different to any violent or active remedies, and require no alteration of diet or confinement. The following respectable testimony in their favour is addressed to the proprietors: - 'Gentlemen, for three years I was affected with indigestion, heartburn, loss of appetite, and dreadful swimming in the head, together with general lowness of spirits to such a degree that I was unable at intervals to attend to business. After consulting many able psychiatrists, and taking much medicine in vain, I had recourse to your pills and have found in the use of them permanent relief.'

The Morning Chronicle, **Saturday 4 May 1822**
(v.52, p.4)

~

MIDDLESEX SESSIONS,

THURSDAY, JULY 11

TRIAL OF BENBOW

William Benbow was indicted for publishing certain obscene libels. The indictment contained

12 counts, ten of which contained extracts from a Magazine and Novel published by the defendant, and the other two described prints contained in these works.

Mr. Adolphus stated the case for the prosecution. He said the prosecution was instituted by the Society for the Suppression of Vice against the defendant, not for one, but for a persevering publication of libels. In the beginning of the present year, the defendant, who had kept a large shop in the Strand, removed to Castle-street, Leicester-square, where he commenced the publication of a periodical work, called 'The Rambler's Magazine'; passages from which formed some of the counts in the indictment. In the fourth number of the Magazine he announced that he was about to publish a French Novel, which was out of print, without curtailment, in two pocket volumes, at the low price of 6d a number, and gave a specimen of the work. The work, as they would feel when they heard the indictment read, contained some passages most inflammatory to the passions of youth.

[NOTE: William Benbow successfully defended himself against the accusations made by the

Society for the Suppression of Vice, and managed to publish *The Amours of the Chevalier de Faublas*. Though not utterly pornographic, the text is in places racy. At one point in the second volume our hero (the Chevalier himself) is imprisoned by nuns beneath a convent and left overnight with a single nun to pray for his soul. Urbanely, the Chevalier observes that 'If ever seduction was excusable, most assuredly this is the case'. However, rather than an account of the subterranean peccadilloes, the author prefers to: 'Let the curious bishop who shalt devoutly peruse this wicked book when alone by his fireside, [...] if he possess as warm an imagination as its young author, compose what ought to fill the next six pages.' No stranger to infamy, Benbow was also credited with disinterring the bones of Thomas Paine. *The Amours of the Chevalier de Faublas, new and faithfully translated from the Paris edition of 1821*: London, 1822, vol. 2, p.195.]

The Morning Chronicle, **Friday 12 July 1822**
(v.53, p.127)

Literary Libelling
Scotch Jury Court, Edinburgh, July 22
           Professor Leslie *v.* Blackwood.

This Highly important case excited a great deal of
interest, and the court was crowded at an early hour.

The substance of the issues against the defender
was, whether, in various numbers of *Blackwood's
Magazine*, the pursuer is falsely accused,
maliciously, and injuriously represented, and held
up to ridicule and contempt as being a plagiary, to
the injury and damage of the pursuer?

Whether the pursuer is falsely, maliciously, and
injuriously represented, and held up to public
ridicule and contempt, by representing him to be,
or asserting that he is, an insolent dogmatist; or
that he has the impudence to criticise that of which
he is ignorant, or that he actuated by hostility to
the language of revelation, simply because it is the
language of revelation; or as being lying, dishonest,
or joining with a bookseller to impose upon the
public by dishonesty; or as having purloined
from other authors; or as having been guilty of a

thousand *betises*; or as resembling a parrot.

Whether the pursuer is falsely, maliciously, and injuriously represented, and held out and represented as being one of the public teachers, by whom young men who come as students to the University of Edinburgh have their religious principles perverted and their reverence for holy things sneered away, to the injury and damage of said pursuer.

The damages were laid at 5,000l.

The Times, **Saturday 27 July 1822 (v.53, p.172)**

A large fish, of the whale species denominated a finner, was seen by several persons on Sunday last, sporting in the deep, 10 or 12 miles from the land, off the mouth of the Tees and the Yorkshire coast. It appeared to be from 60 to 70 feet long. It repeatedly made its appearance on the surface of the sea, and as it rose was heard to snort loudly, while the water flew an almost incredible height from its nostrils.

Liverpool Mercury, **Friday 30 August 1822 (v.53, p.287)**

A professional Gentleman of some eminence at Preston, we understand, intending to leave home during the Guild, determined to let his house, asking for the use of it during the festival the sum of 300 guineas. A lady applied to take it, but was told, as she was a stranger, the proprietor would require the sum of 150 guineas in advance. This was complied with, and she has been admitted to possession; since which, to his infinite mortification, the owner of the house has discovered that she is no other than a lady of easy virtue.

The Morning Chronicle, **Thursday 5 September 1822 (v.54, p.61)**

❖

GROG – until the time of Admiral Vernon, the British sailors had their allowance of brandy or rum served out to them unmixed with water. This plan was found to be attended with inconvenience on some occasions; and the Admiral, therefore, ordered in the fleet that he commanded, the spirit should always be mixed with water before it was given to the men. This innovation, at first, gave great offence to the sailors, and rendered the commander very unpopular. The admiral, at that time, wore a grogram coat, and was nicknamed 'Old Grog'. This name was afterwards given to the mixed liquor he compelled them to take; and it has since universally obtained the name of grog.

Caledonian Mercury, **Monday 2 December 1822**
(v.55, p.36)

~

ERRATUM

THE LATE MR. HOWARD
We beg leave to correct an error that occurred in the REVIEW of last Sunday, relative to this gentleman, in which he was stated to be *unjustly*, instead of *most justly* celebrated for his humanity.

Courier and *Evening Gazette*, **January 1799 (v.14, p.15)**

In a London paper, of the last week, is the following curious apology for a hasty accusation – 'A paragraph in our last paper, rather precipitously accuses, with ingratitude, a gentleman who gave *two-pence* as a reward to a waterman for risking his life in saving a lady who had fallen in the River; but had the writer of that paragraph been acquainted with all the particulars, he probably would have suppressed his censure. – The lady to whom the accident happened was the gentleman's *wife*.

Public Advertiser, Friday 20 August 1790 (v.5, p.56)

Visit our website and discover thousands
of other History Press books.

www.thehistorypress.co.uk